Level 11, Unit 1 ENTERPRISES

SKILLS INDEX

Name _____ Date _____

Read the sentences. Use context clues to choose the best meaning for each underlined word. Circle the letter of the meaning you choose.

1. My mother is an avid follower of yard sales. She will drive twenty miles or more just to attend one.
   a. discouraged
   (b.) enthusiastic
   c. quiet
   d. lazy

2. On Saturday morning, she perused the newspaper and discovered that four yard sales were to be held in our town alone.
   a. picked up
   b. wrote to
   (c.) read carefully
   d. threw out

3. Mom asked me if I'd come with her. I would rather have stayed home, but I could see she wanted company. Reluctantly, I said I'd go along.
   a. eagerly
   b. fortunately
   c. bitterly
   (d.) unwillingly

4. At the first sale, we saw a rusty rack of old garments. They looked as if they hadn't been worn by anyone for fifty years.
   (a.) clothes
   b. books
   c. tools
   d. toys

5. But then I spotted a unique ring on a table. What was so unusual about the ring was that it was engraved with my initials: PQZ.
   a. ordinary
   b. ugly
   c. weird
   (d.) one of a kind

6. The price tag on the ring read $4. I showed it to Mom, and she suggested I buy it. She guessed its true value was much higher.
   (a.) worth
   b. bargain
   c. weight
   d. metal

7. I paid for the ring and tried it on at once. I anxiously anticipate the next yard sale and the hidden treasures I might find there.
   a. avoid
   b. dread
   (c.) look forward to
   d. plan

"Kid Power," *Landscapes* (Hardcover: pages 18-32) *Enterprises* (Softcover: pages 10-24)

Objective: Define words using context clues *(Comprehension and Vocabulary Skills)*

Extension: Have students circle the clue words in each sentence that helped them to identify the meaning of the word.

1

Name _____   Date _____

A. Read the definitions. Then match a word from the box with its definition and write it on the lines below. Not all the words will be used, and the word in the puzzle box is what people in business hope to make.

slogan	publicity	investments	profit	merchandise	enterprise

1. sums of money that are put into a business
2. the amount remaining after all the costs of a business have been paid
3. a phrase used to advertise a product
4. a project that is difficult or important
5. information to attract public attention to something

1. i n v e s t **m** e n t s
2. p r **o** f i t
3. s l o g a **n**
4. e n t **e** r p r i s e
5. p u b l i c i t **y**

B. Read each sentence. Circle the letter next to the word that best completes each sentence.

1. The fifth grade's _____ was to organize a fair to raise money for their school.
   a. profit   **(b.)** enterprise   **c.** slogan   **d.** investment

2. Karen was in charge of _____, so she placed ads in several newspapers.
   a. merchandise   **(b.)** publicity   **c.** enterprise   **d.** slogan

3. She thought up a clever _____ for the event: "Our fair will fairly surprise you."
   a. publicity   **b.** enterprise   **c.** profit   **(d.)** slogan

4. The _____ made from the fair will go toward the building of a new playing field for the school.
   (a.) profit   **b.** merchandise   **c.** slogan   **d.** publicity

"Kid Power," *Landscapes* (Hardcover: pages 18-32) *Enterprises* (Softcover: pages 10-24)
Objective: Use vocabulary words *(Comprehension and Vocabulary Skills)*
Extension: Have students write three sentences using the following word pairs: *merchandise, publicity; investments, profit; slogan, enterprise.*
2

Name   Date

A. Explain the role played by each of these characters in "Kid Power." (Answers will vary.)

1. Janie Golden   Janie was a young girl who started a business, "Kid Power," in order

to earn money to buy a bike.

2. Carol Golden   Carol was Janie's sister; she contributed to Kid Power by making signs

and baking cookies.

3. Mrs. Dale   Mrs. Dale hired Janie to watch the children of adults who came to her

yard sale.

4. Mrs. Marks   Mrs. Marks hired Janie to model the clothes she was making for her

granddaughter who lived in Oregon.

B. Use complete sentences to answer these questions about "Kid Power."

1. How did Janie first advertise her new business?

She put up a sign on the bulletin board at the supermarket.

2. Why did Mrs. Marks want to know Janie's dress size?

Mrs. Marks needed to know if Janie wore the same size as her granddaughter.

3. What did Janie do with Carol's cookies at the yard sale?

She gave the cookies to the children; she sold them for a nickel apiece to the adults.

4. Do you agree with Mrs. Dale's comment that Janie will be a millionaire by the time she's twenty-one? Why or why not?

Answers will vary but students should realize that Janie will probably not be a millionaire by

age twenty-one; it's extremely unusual for anyone to earn a million dollars at such an early

age. But, Janie may have been involved in several successful business ventures by then.

She's enterprising and will have learned how to make a profit.

"Kid Power," *Landscapes* **(Hardcover: pages 18-32)** *Enterprises* **(Softcover: pages 10-24)**

Objective: Demonstrate story comprehension *(Comprehension and Vocabulary Skills)*

Name _____ Date _____

A. Read the words below. Then underline the suffix in each word.

-ar, -er, -or = one who _____; of or like
-ist = one who does or makes; one who believes or practices

pianist   winner   collector   cyclist   elevator

photographer   bicyclist   cartoonist   angular   waiter

actor   decorator   stellar   conductor   naturalist

astronomer   harpist   juggler   navigator   triangular

B. Read the story below. Then use the words above to complete each sentence. (Note: Not all the words from Part A will be used, and each word will only be used once.)

Last summer I accompanied Mom on a business trip to California. On the five-hour flight, I met a professional _____ bicyclist _____ who had his bicycle shipped separately. He was a first place _____ winner _____ in the 1985 _____ cyclist _____ contest held in Toronto, Canada. During the flight we hit some stormy weather, but the stewardess assured us that the pilot was an excellent _____ navigator _____.

Our first dinner in San Francisco was in a _____ triangular _____ building with three sides and three floors! In the lobby, we were greeted by the music of a _____ pianist _____ and a _____ harpist _____. After reading the restaurant's directory, Mom suggested that we take the _____ elevator _____ to the second floor. The interior _____ decorator _____ for this floor must have been a true _____ naturalist _____ because the room's decor made us feel as if we were outdoors! Even the ceiling was lit by small _____ angular _____ lights illuminating the room from all angles. We were sure that an _____ astronomer _____ was consulted before these stars were placed in position. There was so much to look at and listen to that when our _____ waiter _____ came to take our order, we hadn't even looked at our menus!

MACMILLAN PUBLISHING COMPANY

"Kid Power," *Landscapes* (Hardcover: pages 18-32) *Enterprises* (Softcover: pages 10-24)

Objective: Identify suffixes: *-ar, -er, -or, -ist* (Decoding and Phonics Skills)

Extension: Have students write a paragraph using as many of the unused words from Part A as possible.

Name   Date

Use the sample dictionary page to answer the questions below. Circle the letter of each answer.

---

panel   **parapet**

pan·el (pan′ əl) *n.* **1.** a flat piece forming part of a surface on a wall or elsewhere. **2.** a board containing instruments or controls. **3.** a group of people gathered to discuss an issue.

pang (pang) *n.* a sharp, sudden feeling of pain or distress: *pangs of hunger.*

par·a·gon (pãr′ ə gon′) *n.* a perfect model.

par·a·lyze (pãr′ ə līz′) *v.* **par·a·lyzed, par·a·lyz·ing. 1.** to stop the ability to move or feel in a bodily part. **2.** to make powerless.

a bat,	**ā** cake,	**ä** father,	**är** car,	**ãr** dare;	**e** hen,	**ē** me,
ėr term;	**i** bib,	**ī** kite,	**ir** clear;	**o** top,	**ō** rope,	**ô** saw,
oi coin,	**ôr** fork,	**ou** out;	**u** sun,	**u̇** book,	**ü** moon,	**ū** cute;
ə about,	taken					

1. What part of speech is the word *panel*?
   a. verb   **b.** adjective   (**c.**) noun   **d.** adverb

2. Which definition of *panel* is used in the sentence below?
   The panel disagreed about the best way to invest one's money.
   a. 1   **b.** 2   (**c.**) 3   **d.** none of the above

3. Which word in the pronunciation key tells you how to pronounce *a* in pang?
   (**a.**) bat   **b.** car   **c.** cake   **d.** about

4. What is the meaning of *pang*?
   a. a hit   **b.** a model
   (**c.**) a painful feeling   **d.** a pleasant feeling

5. Which syllable of *paralyze* is said with the most stress?
   (**a.**) first   **b.** third
   c. second   **d.** none of the above

6. Which of the following word groups can be found on this dictionary page?
   a. parka, panic, panther   **b.** parallel, paradox, parrot
   c. paper, papa, parent   (**d.**) parade, paramedic, paradise

---

"Kid Power," *Landscapes* (Hardcover: pages 18-32) *Enterprises* (Softcover: pages 10-24)

Objective: Use the dictionary: guide words, definitions, pronunciation key, part of speech *(Study Skills)*

Extension: Have students illustrate the three meanings of *panel* as defined on this page. Then have them write a sentence describing each illustration.

5

Name _____ Date _____

Read each paragraph. Circle the letter of the sentence below that best summarizes the paragraph.

1. All four of the kids in my family work. My brother Ron has a newspaper route. His delivery area covers several neighborhoods. My sister Bonnie babysits three nights a week. My other sister, Kim, collects old soda bottles. Then she turns them in at the local supermarket for a nickel a bottle. As for me, I do yard work for five of our neighbors. I mow their lawns in the summer while they are on vacation. In the winter, I shovel the snow from their driveways.

   a. My sister Bonnie babysits several nights each week.

   b. Whatever the season, I prefer to work outdoors.

   (c.) All the kids in my family have some kind of job: Ron delivers papers, Bonnie babysits, Kim collects bottles, and I do yard work.

   d. Besides me, there are three children in my family: Ron, my brother, and Bonnie and Kim, my sisters.

2. Ron used to dread delivering the newspaper to Mrs. Fratti's house. She has a large, black dog named Shep, whom she usually keeps tied up by the garage. Whenever Ron approached the house, Shep would bark furiously. Ron was sure that if Shep ever got loose, he'd be in big trouble. One day, as Ron neared Mrs. Fratti's house, he saw Shep sitting on the front stoop. The dog was not barking. In fact, Ron thought he saw the dog's tail wagging. Ron debated whether or not he should toss the paper up to the stoop from the sidewalk. He decided against doing such a thing. Instead, he walked slowly up to Mrs. Fratti's front door. Was Ron ever surprised when Shep sat up and begged as he rang Mrs. Fratti's bell. All Shep wanted was to be allowed inside the house!

   a. Mrs. Fratti usually kept her dog Shep tied up by the garage.

   (b.) Ron used to be afraid of Mrs. Fratti's dog until he learned that all Shep wanted was to be let inside the house.

   c. Ron debated whether or not he should toss the paper onto the stoop, but he decided that Mrs. Fratti probably wouldn't appreciate that very much.

   d. Ron used to dread delivering Mrs. Fratti's paper, but now he doesn't mind doing it.

"You Can Get a Job!" *Landscapes* (Hardcover: pages 34-41) *Enterprises* (Softcover: pages 26-33)

Objective: Summarize a paragraph *(Comprehension and Vocabulary Skills)*

Extension: Have students write a short paragraph describing a job they have or would like to have. Then have them summarize the paragraph in one sentence.

6

Name _____ Date _____

A. Read the story. Then use words from the box to complete the sentences.

chore	rate	errands	employer
permit	negotiating	recommendation	consumer

It was Roberto's first day on the job, and he wanted to please his

_____employer_____, Mr. Chin. Mr. Chin owned a flower shop. He was

paying Roberto a good _____rate_____ for a beginner on the job

because Roberto had come with a good _____recommendation_____ from his last

employer. All morning Roberto ran _____errands_____ for his new boss.
By noon, he felt he was earning every penny of his pay. Roberto was exhausted

and hoped Mr. Chin would _____permit_____ him to take an hour
for lunch.

But before Roberto could say anything, Mr. Chin came up to him and said, "I

have one more _____chore_____ for you, Roberto."

Roberto's heart sank. He was so hungry that he felt like _____negotiating_____
with Mr. Chin. Then Mr. Chin smiled. "I want you to take this money and go
across the street to buy us each a big sandwich and something to drink," he
said. "After all, it's lunchtime."

Roberto grinned. He was going to like working for Mr. Chin after all.

_____

B. Use each pair of words in a sentence. (Sentences will vary.)

1. consumer/rate _____

_____

2. permit/negotiating _____

_____

3. recommendation/employer _____

_____

Name _____   Date _____

A. Read the following statements about "You <u>Can</u> Get a Job!" If the statement is true, write **True.** If the statement is false, write **False.** Then in complete sentences write the reasons for your answers. (Reasons will vary.)

1. Most kids first work for people they know, such as parents and neighbors.

   True. Most kids first work for people they know, because these people know them and

   trust them.

2. A good way to handle the pay rate for a job is to wait several weeks after you've started and then talk to your employer.

   False. A good way to handle the pay rate for a job is to discuss it with your employer

   before you start work.

3. It helps to practice a job before you start doing it for money.

   True. It helps to practice a job so that you will be sure of doing it the right way.

4. Many of the kids who wrote to *Penny Power* about their jobs were looking for new jobs.

   False. Most of the kids who wrote said they'd like to continue doing the jobs they had.

B. Each quotation in Column A is from "You <u>Can</u> Get a Job!" Decide which job from Column B is described in the quotation. Write the letter of the job on the line after each quotation.

Column A

1. "Try to avoid doing this job! You get splinters." ___c___

2. "You should like little kids and meet them before

   you start the job." ___a___

3. "Don't skip corners. Be careful of flowers." ___d___

4. "My friend had it. Then my brother. Then my

   other brother and now me." ___b___

Column B

a. babysitting

b. delivering newspapers

c. cutting wood

d. mowing lawns

"You <u>Can</u> Get a Job!" *Landscapes* (Hardcover: pages 34-41) *Enterprises* (Softcover: pages 26-33)

Objective: Demonstrate story comprehension *(Comprehension and Vocabulary Skills)*

Name _____ Date _____

Read each group of four sentences. Three of the sentences state facts. One states an opinion. Put a check next to the statement of opinion.

1. _____ A consumer is anyone who buys and uses up things offered for sale.

   _____ Young people, as well as adults, are consumers.

   _____ There are two kinds of businesses: those that sell products and those that provide services.

   ✔ It's more important to provide people with services than it is to sell them goods.

2. _____ Indianapolis is the capital and largest city in Indiana.

   _____ No other state west of the Appalachian Mountains is smaller than Indiana, except Hawaii.

   ✔ People who live in Indiana are friendlier than people in neighboring states.

   _____ Indiana is located in the north-central United States.

3. _____ The parrot is an example of a tropical bird.

   ✔ It is cruel to keep any kind of bird as a pet.

   _____ Some parrots can imitate human speech.

   _____ *Parrakeet* is another spelling of *parakeet*.

4. _____ The parts of a mobile are hung from thin wires and set in motion by air currents.

   _____ Alexander Calder was not only a sculptor; he was also a creator of mobiles.

   _____ The mobiles of Alexander Calder have been exhibited at the Solomon R. Guggenheim Museum in New York City.

   ✔ Because they have moving parts, mobiles are more interesting than other kinds of sculpture.

"You Can Get a Job!" *Landscapes* (Hardcover: pages 34-41) *Enterprises* (Softcover: pages 26-33)

Objective: Identify facts and opinions (*Comprehension and Vocabulary Skills*)

Extension: Have students choose one group of sentences on the page and write one fact and one opinion that could be added to it.

9

Name _____ Date _____

Read each selection. Then circle the letter of the phrase that best completes each numbered sentence.

Professor Windblow prepared to show his new computer to the roomful of scientists. He pressed the "on" button, but nothing happened. He checked out the computer's system, and everything seemed in order. He gave the machine a jiggle with his hand. Still nothing happened. Then the absent-minded professor gazed down at the empty wall socket and smiled. He went around to the back of the computer. When he returned, the computer's lights were flashing, and it was humming softly.

1. You can conclude that _____.

   a. something was wrong with the "on" button

   b. the computer wasn't finished

   (c.) Professor Windblow had forgotten to plug in the computer

   d. the computer needed time to warm up

2. One clue that pointed to this conclusion was _____.

   (a.) the empty wall socket   **b.** the roomful of scientists

   c. the flashing lights on the computer   **d.** the pressing of the "on" button

Mrs. Kramer opened the breadbox and looked with surprise at the loaves of cranberry bread. Half of one loaf was missing! Just then little Ralphie entered the kitchen. As he reached for the refrigerator door, Mrs. Kramer noticed that his fingers were unusually red. "What do you think you're doing?" asked Mrs. Kramer.

"Getting something to eat," answered Ralphie.

"You can't possibly be hungry still!" his mother said firmly.

Little Ralphie sighed. He knew he'd been caught.

3. Mrs. Kramer wouldn't let Ralphie have food because _____.

   a. she was saving the food for company

   (b.) he had already eaten a half a loaf of cranberry bread

   c. it was almost time for supper

   d. she wanted him to take a nap

4. One clue that gave Ralphie away was _____.

   a. the bread box   **b.** the way he answered his mother

   c. the way he sighed   **(d.)** his red fingers

"The Doughnut Machine," *Landscapes* (Hardcover: pages 46-58) *Enterprises* (Softcover: pages 38-50)

Objective: Draw conclusions *(Comprehension and Vocabulary Skills)*   **Extension:** Have students underline two other clues in the first paragraph that led to the conclusion they selected.

Name _____ Date _____

A. Read the clues. Then write words from the box to complete the puzzle.

automatic	market	profession	devices	gadget	mechanical

ACROSS

1. an occupation requiring special training
2. of or involving machines
3. operating by itself

DOWN

2. a demand for something
4. a small mechanical device
5. things made for a special purpose

1. ACROSS: p r o f e s s i o n

2. ACROSS: m e c h a n i c a l

3. ACROSS: a u t o m a t i c

5. DOWN: d e v i c e s

4. DOWN: g a d g e t

2. DOWN: m a r k e t

_____

B. Read the sentences below. Then use the words from the box above to complete each sentence.

1. Jay is very _____mechanical_____ and can fix just about anything that breaks.

2. I don't feel there is much of a _____market_____ now for doughnuts without holes.

3. The _____automatic_____ toaster turns out perfect toast with just a flick of a switch.

4. Many taffy producers use a machine with special _____devices_____ that rotate and pull the taffy.

5. Elena would like to be a doctor like her father and join the medical _____profession_____.

6. I wonder what newfangled _____gadget_____ Pierre will invent next.

"The Doughnut Machine," *Landscapes* (Hardcover: pages 46-58) *Enterprises* (Softcover: pages 38-50)

Objective: Use vocabulary words *(Comprehension and Vocabulary Skills)*

Extension: Have students write a paragraph using the words in the box in Part A.

Name   Date

A. The events described below are about "The Doughnut Machine." Number the events in the order in which they happened.

___4___ Homer couldn't shut the doughnut machine off.

___8___ The lady returned to the lunch room for her bracelet.

___6___ People gathered outside to look at all the doughnuts.

___2___ Mr. Gabby came into the lunch room for some doughnuts.

___7___ Mr. Gabby was hired to advertise doughnuts.

___1___ Uncle Ulysses asked Homer to fix the doughnut machine.

___9___ Rupert Black found the bracelet inside the doughnut.

___5___ Homer telephoned Uncle Ulysses for help.

___3___ The rich lady helped Homer make doughnuts.

B. Read the questions below. Then use complete sentences to answer each question about "The Doughnut Machine." (Answers will vary.)

1. What did Mr. Gabby do for a living?

He walked around with a sandwich board, advertising different things.

2. What mistake did the lady make in preparing the doughnuts?

She used too much batter.

3. Where was Uncle Ulysses while the doughnut machine was making all the doughnuts?

He was playing cards with the sheriff at the barber shop.

4. Why did the lady return to the lunch room?

She returned to find her missing diamond bracelet.

5. What do you think the signs that Homer thought up to sell all the doughnuts said?

Answers will vary but students should mention that there is a $100 reward for finding

a diamond bracelet in a doughnut.

"**The Doughnut Machine,**" *Landscapes* (Hardcover: pages 46-58) *Enterprises* (Softcover: pages 38-50)

Objective: Demonstrate story comprehension *(Comprehension and Vocabulary Skills)*

Name _____   Date _____

A. Each sentence below contains an idiom or an example of hyperbole. Decide which phrase below the sentence best explains its meaning. Then fill in the circle of the letter next to the best answer.

1. The crowd of customers was <u>hungry enough to have eaten the entire lunch room</u>.
   - (a) filled and satisfied
   - (b) starved
   - (c) slightly hungry
   - (d) sick of doughnuts

2. The rich lady <u>raised the roof</u> when she learned that her diamond bracelet was missing.
   - (a) removed the building's roof
   - (b) was very upset
   - (c) laughed and sang
   - (d) tore down the lunch room

3. Uncle Ulysses <u>burned the midnight oil</u> trying to think of new ways to improve his restaurant.
   - (a) started a fire
   - (b) failed
   - (c) worked till very late
   - (d) conducted experiments

4. Homer <u>could sleep through a four-alarm fire</u>.
   - (a) was a light sleeper
   - (b) was a deep sleeper
   - (c) didn't fall asleep easily
   - (d) was a sleepwalker

5. Mr. Gabby didn't mind waiting for the doughnuts because he <u>had time on his hands</u>.
   - (a) wore a wristwatch
   - (b) was very lazy
   - (c) had nothing else to do
   - (d) didn't know the time

B. The first sentence below contains an idiom. The second contains an example of hyperbole. Rewrite each sentence, using only literal language. (Wording will vary.)

1. The rich lady cut no corners in making her famous doughnuts.

   The rich lady took no shortcuts in making her famous doughnuts.

2. Homer felt two inches tall when Uncle Ulysses saw the mess he'd made of his lunch room.

   Homer felt bad when Uncle Ulysses saw the mess he'd made of his lunch room.

"The Doughnut Machine," *Landscapes* (Hardcover: pages 46-58) *Enterprises* (Softcover: pages 38-50)

Objective: Interpret figurative language: simile, metaphor, idiom, hyperbole *(Literature and Language Skills)*

Extension: Have students write a sentence using the following idioms: *to the letter, steal his thunder, once in a blue moon.* Then have them rewrite each sentence using literal language.

Name _____ Date _____

Read the following sentences. Then circle the letter next to the best meaning for each underlined word.

1. The man set up his <u>tripod</u> and snapped a picture of the new restaurant.
   (a.) stand for a camera   **b.** canvas
   c. notebook   **d.** chair

2. The <u>recipe</u> for the dish called for three eggs and a cup of milk.
   a. note   **(b.)** instructions for cooking
   c. bowl   **d.** a kind of food

3. We quickly put all the <u>perishable</u> foods into the refrigerator.
   a. good-tasting   **b.** instant
   c. canned   **(d.)** easily spoiled

4. Sally eats only natural foods. She wouldn't touch anything containing <u>artificial</u> flavors.
   a. real   **b.** strong
   c. cheap   **(d.)** made by humans

5. The machine made a <u>duplicate</u> of my paper. I gave the original to my teacher.
   a. picture   **b.** mess
   (c.) copy   **d.** improvement

6. I <u>yearn</u> for a machine that will do my homework for me.
   (a.) wish longingly   **b.** plan
   c. fear greatly   **d.** will not wait

7. Frank took a class in modern machines at the <u>university</u>.
   a. gym   **b.** hospital
   (c.) large college   **d.** factory

8. There was <u>ample</u> room at the table for all ten people, but it got a little <u>crowded</u> when three more diners arrived.
   a. little   **(b.)** plenty of
   c. some   **d.** no

HOMEWORK MACHINE

Skills Activity: Context Clues, *Landscapes* (Hardcover: pages 60-61) *Enterprises* (Softcover: pages 52-53)

Objective: Define words using context clues *(Comprehension and Vocabulary Skills)*

Extension: Have students look up and write a sentence containing context clues for each of the following words: *feat, forge, lark, muse, wary.*

14

Name _____   Date _____

A. The statements below are based on "The Toothpaste Millionaire." If a statement is a fact, write **F**. If it is an opinion, write **O**.

___F___ **1.** Joe Smiley is the host of a TV talk show.

___O___ **2.** Joe Smiley's show is one of the best on TV.

___O___ **3.** Most toothpastes are far too expensive.

___F___ **4.** Rufus got the idea for making toothpaste while shopping for his mother.

___F___ **5.** Rufus' commercial for *Toothpaste* was short and to the point.

___O___ **6.** The people who make commercials could learn a lot from Rufus Mayflower.

___F___ **7.** Kate bought fifty gross of aluminum tubes for Rufus' toothpaste.

___O___ **8.** The aluminum tubes were incredibly cheap.

___O___ **9.** Mr. Perkell of Everybody's Friendly Bank should have loaned Rufus the money he needed.

___F___ **10.** *Toothpaste* made Rufus Mayflower a millionaire.

B. Read each pair of sentences. Then underline the one sentence that states an opinion.

1. Toothpaste was first sold in little baby jars.
2. This was the wrong way to package a product like toothpaste.

1. Everyone should own shares of stock in businesses they think will be successful.
2. At the end of the year, each stockholder gets a share of the year's profits.

1. Dr. Rodriguez, a dentist, recommends the use of dental floss.
2. It's more important to use dental floss than it is to brush your teeth.

1. Each year some companies go out of business because they are not profitable.
2. Businesses should not be allowed to earn large profits.

"The Toothpaste Millionaire," *Landscapes* **(Hardcover: pages 62-76)** *Enterprises* **(Softcover: pages 54-68)**

Objective: Identify facts and opinions *(Comprehension and Vocabulary Skills)*

Extension: Have students reword the four sentences in Part B that are opinions so that they are factual statements.

15

Name _____   Date _____

A. Read the definitions. Then match a word from the box with its definition and write it on the lines below. Not all the words will be used, and the word in the puzzle box will tell you what toothpaste adds a sparkle to.

salary	commercials	interview	stock	initiative	portable

1. shares in a company
2. advertising messages on radio or television
3. the ability to take a first step in doing something
4. a sum of money paid to someone for regular work
5. a meeting between a writer or reporter and a person from whom information is wanted

1. _s t o c k_
2. _c o m m e r c i a l s_
3. _i n i t i a t i v e_
4. _s a l a r y_
5. _i n t e r v i e w_

B. Use each word below in a sentence. (Sentences will vary.)

1. portable _____

_____

2. stock _____

_____

3. interview _____

_____

4. salary _____

_____

MACMILLAN PUBLISHING COMPANY

"The Toothpaste Millionaire," *Landscapes* **(Hardcover: pages 62-76)** *Enterprises* **(Softcover: pages 54-68)**

Objective: Use vocabulary words *(Comprehension and Vocabulary Skills)*

Extension: Have students write one sentence using the following words: *commercials, initiative.*

Name _____   Date _____

A. Each quotation in Column 1 is from the play "The Toothpaste Millionaire." Match the quotation with the character in Column 2. Write the letter of your choice on the line.

Column 1   **Column 2**

__b__ **1.** "Isn't he *fantastic*?"   **a.** Hector

__d__ **2.** "I have a friend who needs a certain kind of   **b.** Joe Smiley
machine for filling toothpaste tubes."   **c.** Mr. Conti

__e__ **3.** "Well, I wasn't trying to make money, just to   **d.** Kate MacKinstrey
make toothpaste."   **e.** Rufus Mayflower

__a__ **4.** "I was a mechanic for the Happy Lips Lotion
Company."

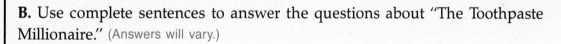

__c__ **5.** "All right, class, take out your math books."

B. Use complete sentences to answer the questions about "The Toothpaste Millionaire." (Answers will vary.)

1. Who helped Rufus package and sell *Toothpaste*?

His classmates, Kate, Josie, Lee Lu, and Clem, helped him.

_____

2. How did Kate's brother James help her get toothpaste tubes?

He told her about an auction at which 50 gross of aluminum tubes were to be sold.

_____

3. Why do you think Mr. Perkell, the banker, turned Rufus down when he asked for a loan?

Answers will vary, but students should mention that he probably turned Rufus down because

Rufus was so young and had no previous business experience.

4. What product might you be able to produce and sell more cheaply than anyone else?

_____

"The Toothpaste Millionaire," *Landscapes* (Hardcover: pages 62-76) *Enterprises* (Softcover: pages 54-68)

Objective: Demonstrate story comprehension *(Comprehension and Vocabulary Skills)*

Name   Date

Use the sample dictionary page to answer the questions below. Fill in the circle next to the letter of each answer.

---

studio   **system**

stu · di · o (stü′ dē ō′) *n.* **1.** an artist's workroom. **2.** a school where arts are taught or studied. **3.** a room or building for movie or TV production.

su · perb (sü perb′) *adj.* of the highest quality.

swerve (swurv) *v.* **swerved, swerving.** to turn aside sharply from a straight course.

sym · pa · thet · ic (sim′ pə thet′ ik) *adj.* **1.** expressing feelings of pity or or sorrow for another. **2.** in agreement.

---

at;   āpe;   cär;   end;   mē;   it;   īce;   hot;   ōld;   fôrk; put;   rüle;   cūte;   oil;   out;   up;   turn;   sing;   thin; this;   hw in white;   zh in treasure.   The symbol ə stands for the sound of a in about, e in taken, i in pencil, o in lemon, and u in circus.

---

1. Which word in the pronunciation key tells you how to pronounce the *i* in *studio*?
   (a) it   (b) end   (c) ice   **(d) me**

2. Which definition of *studio* is used in the following sentence?
To finish the painting, Mr. James worked in his studio all through the night.
   (a) 1   (b) 3   (c) 2   (d) none of the above

3. What does *superb* mean?
   (a) of the lowest quality   **(b) of the highest quality**
   (c) very funny   (d) serious

4. What part of speech is *swerve*?
   (a) noun   (b) adjective   **(c) verb**   (d) adverb

5. Which of these entry words could appear on the sample dictionary page?
   (a) stockade   (b) signature   (c) Szechuan   **(d) symphony**

6. Which word in the pronunciation key tells you how to pronounce the *th* in *sympathetic*?
   (a) thin   (b) this   (c) taken   (d) white

"The Toothpaste Millionaire," *Landscapes* **(Hardcover: pages 62-76)** *Enterprises* **(Softcover: pages 54-68)**

Objective: Use the dictionary: guide words, definitions, pronunciation key, part of speech *(Study Skills)*

Extension: Have students write three sentences, each with a different use of the word *studio.*

Name _____   Date _____

Use words from the box to finish the selection. Use each word only once. Write the words on the numbered lines below the selection.

salary	market	merchandise	stock	consumers	commercials
profit	gadget	recommendation	slogan	publicity	initiative

It takes real __(1)__ to start your own business. It also takes a keen knowledge of what kind of __(2)__ people want to buy. Your product could be anything from a new kind of dog food to some little household __(3)__. But whatever it is, there must be a __(4)__ for it, or you won't be able to sell it.

When you start your business, don't expect to make a __(5)__ the first year, or even the second. It may take a long time before you can even pay yourself a regular __(6)__. All the money you make might have to go back into keeping the business running. To keep going, you may have to sell __(7)__ in your company to interested investors.

Another important thing you'll need to do is inform __(8)__ about your product. The best way to do this is through good __(9)__. If you can afford it, you could run one-minute __(10)__ on television and radio. A catchy __(11)__ spoken by a good actor will make people remember your product the next time they're shopping. You may even want to get a __(12)__ from a famous person who's tried your product and liked it.

1. _____initiative_____   2. _____merchandise_____

3. _____gadget_____   4. _____market_____

5. _____profit_____   6. _____salary_____

7. _____stock_____   8. _____consumers_____

9. _____publicity_____   10. _____commercials_____

11. _____slogan_____   12. _____recommendation_____

Cumulative Vocabulary Review

Objective: Use vocabulary words *(Comprehension and Vocabulary Skills)*

Extension: Have students write a paragraph using as many vocabulary words on this page as possible.

19

Name _____   Date _____

Read each group of four sentences. Three of the sentences state facts. One states an opinion. Put a check next to the statement of opinion.

1. _____ At an auction, an item is sold to the highest bidder.

   ✔ A public auction is the best way to sell unwanted merchandise.

   _____ A professional auctioneer can be entertaining as well as useful.

   _____ Mrs. Orlando made a profit of $13,500 from the auction of the contents of her house.

2. ✔ Television commercials are a complete waste of time.

   _____ This commercial runs for exactly thirty-five seconds.

   _____ Commercials attempt to convince consumers to buy particular products.

   _____ One technique used in some commercials is the testimonial.

3. _____ A famous actress was interviewed last night on television.

   _____ She was asked to describe the most memorable incident in her career.

   _____ A clip from one of her recent movies was shown.

   ✔ She wore an absolutely outrageous outfit.

4. _____ A lemming is a rodent that lives in arctic regions.

   _____ The behavior of lemmings has long puzzled scientists.

   ✔ It's critical that scientists learn why lemmings behave as they do.

   _____ Lemmings migrate across the land in large numbers; many drown when they reach the sea.

5. _____ Metal money was first used in China more than 4,000 years ago.

   _____ The early American Indians used clam shells for money.

   _____ At one time, English money was made from pieces of wood.

   ✔ Paper money that can be folded is more convenient than coins.

Skills Activity: Facts and Opinions, *Landscapes* **(Hardcover: pages 78-79)** *Enterprises* **(Softcover: pages 70-71)**

Objective: Identify facts and opinions *(Comprehension and Vocabulary Skills)*

Extension: Have students rewrite each sentence on this page that contains an opinion so that it becomes a factual statement.

20

Name

Date

Read each paragraph. Then fill in the circle before the phrase that best completes the sentence.

Sandy took a seat in the auditorium just as the lecture began. The guest speaker's voice was like the droning of a bee. The sun shining through the large windows felt warm and good to Sandy. She closed her eyes as the speaker went on. His voice sounded farther and farther away. Suddenly, Sandy shook her head at the sound of a loud noise. The students all around her were applauding as the lecturer left the stage.

Sandy probably _____.
ⓐ enjoyed the lecture
ⓑ had heard the lecturer's speech before
ⓒ wasn't listening closely
🄳 fell asleep in her seat

Phil heard Marigold barking loudly. He looked out the window and saw the dog jumping up and down by a big tree. Phil had never seen Marigold so excited. Phil ran out into the yard. In between Marigold's barks, Phil heard a faint meowing. He looked up into the tree. There, on one of the lower branches, was a neighbor's terrified cat.

You can probably conclude that _____.
🄰 Marigold has chased a cat up a tree
ⓑ Phil doesn't like cats
ⓒ Marigold is a cat
ⓓ cats like to climb trees

Bob walked into the restaurant and asked for a table. The waiter brought him a menu and filled his water glass. Bob read through the menu with its strange and unusual foods. He finally ordered a chicken dish that was labeled hot and spicy. The waiter brought Bob a pot of tea. When he brought Bob's meal, he placed a pair of chopsticks next to it.

Bob is probably _____.
ⓐ visiting China
🄱 eating at a Chinese restaurant
ⓒ in San Francisco
ⓓ not very hungry

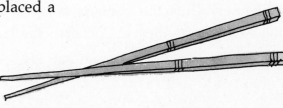

"Henry Reed's Journal," *Landscapes* (Hardcover: pages 80-91) *Enterprises* (Softcover: pages 72-83)

Objective: Draw conclusions *(Comprehension and Vocabulary Skills)*   **Extension:** Have students underline the clues in each paragraph that helped them draw their conclusions.

Name _____ Date _____

A. Read the clues below. Then use the words in the box to complete the crossword puzzle.

edit	lecture	publish	journal	vague	convention

ACROSS

1. to produce printed material for public sale
2. a formal meeting
3. to correct or revise for publication

DOWN

4. a prepared talk on a subject
5. not clearly expressed
6. a daily record of events

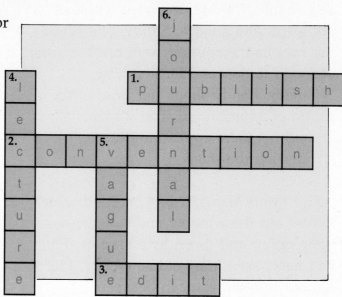

B. Read the story below. Then use the words in the box above to complete the sentences.

   I attended a _____ lecture _____ at a _____ convention _____ held in Chicago last week. The guest speaker was an author who wanted to

_____ publish _____ her latest book. Her book was a _____ journal _____ kept by her grandmother during a trip throughout the continental United States. It was a daily account of comical, interesting, and exciting events occurring in

each state she visited. The author said that there was one _____ vague _____ reference to her grandmother being at the site when the first commercial oil well was drilled near Titusville, Pennsylvania, on August 27, 1859. However, after speaking with her mother, the details were made clearer, and the author had to

_____ edit _____ that chapter considerably before publication.

"Henry Reed's Journal," *Landscapes* (Hardcover: pages 80-91) *Enterprises* (Softcover: pages 72-83)

Objective: Use vocabulary words *(Comprehension and Vocabulary Skills)*

Extension: Have students write a sentence for each of the following word pairs: *journal, vague; publish, edit; lecture, convention.*

22

Name _____ Date _____

A. Use complete sentences to answer the following questions about "Henry Reed's Journal." (Answers will vary.)

1. Why was the Glass family in San Francisco?

   Mr. Glass, a chemist, was attending a convention there.

2. What favor did the woman ask Midge outside the auditorium?

   She asked Midge to watch her dog Amy while she went inside to hear a lecture.

3. What did Amy collect from inside the auditorium?

   She collected and hid the shoes of several people.

4. Henry kept a journal of his trip, and Midge collected curios. What would you do to remember a trip you took?

   _____

   _____

   _____

B. The events listed below are about "Henry Reed's Journal." The events are not in the right order. Number the events in the order in which they occurred.

___7___ Midge noticed that Amy had a different shoe in her mouth.

___5___ Dr. Allison explained how much her dog loves shoes.

___1___ Henry decided to keep a journal of his travels.

___4___ Henry and Midge waited outside the auditorium to see Mr. Glass.

___8___ Dr. Allison announced that Amy had hidden several shoes.

___10___ Henry and Midge went to a movie down the street.

___3___ Henry and Midge read books in the hotel lobby.

___9___ Mr. Glass gave the young people permission to visit Chinatown.

___2___ Midge and her mother met Henry at the airport in San Francisco.

___6___ Henry and Midge agreed to watch Amy for Dr. Allison.

Name _____   Date _____

A. Each of these sentences contains a simile or a metaphor. Decide which phrase best explains the meaning of the figure of speech. Fill in the circle next to your answer.

1. The old shoe tasted like a T-bone steak to the dog.

ⓐ odd   **ⓑ very good**   ⓒ tough   ⓓ sour

2. In the setting sun, the bridge was a ribbon of gold.

ⓐ a golden bridge   ⓑ an unsafe bridge

ⓒ a magic bridge   **ⓓ a bridge glowing with sunlight**

3. The chemist's eyes were two big saucers when his experiment finally succeeded.

ⓐ filled with tears   ⓑ red with anger

ⓒ opened wide with surprise   ⓓ shut tight

4. The little dog worked like lightning, hiding one shoe after another behind the couch.

ⓐ sounded like thunder   ⓑ worked slowly

ⓒ flashed and lit up   **ⓓ worked quickly**

B. Read each sentence. Decide which phrase below might replace the underlined words. Fill in the circle next to your answer.

1. The cat suddenly became very still as the growling dog approached it.

ⓐ turned to stone   ⓑ turned to cotton

ⓒ turned to jelly   ⓓ turned to straw

2. The backyard was wild, unkept, and overrun with weeds.

ⓐ was like a desert   ⓑ was like a mountain

ⓒ was like a jungle   ⓓ was like a river

3. When all the people had finally left, the once-bustling auditorium was extremely quiet.

ⓐ colorful circus   ⓑ an undiscovered tomb

ⓒ a noisy sidewalk   **ⓓ a dark forest**

4. When Jeffrey saw his math test, he was very pleased with himself.

ⓐ as red as a beet   ⓑ as limp as a dishrag

ⓒ as smart as a whip   **ⓓ as proud as a peacock**

MACMILLAN PUBLISHING COMPANY

"Henry Reed's Journal," *Landscapes* **(Hardcover: pages 80-91)** *Enterprises* **(Softcover: pages 72-83)**

Objective: Interpret figurative language: simile, metaphor, idiom, hyperbole *(Literature and Language Skills)*

Extension: Have students select one of the other answer choices in Part B and write sentences using the figures of speech appropriately.

Name   Date

Read each paragraph. Underline the main idea sentence. Then write a summary of the paragraph using complete sentences. (Wording will vary.)

There's much to see on a visit to San Francisco. The city is built on more than forty hills and is nearly surrounded by water. Therefore, there is great natural beauty. There are also fascinating sites, such as the Golden Gate Bridge, which is one of the largest and most spectacular suspension bridges in the world, and Lombard Street, famous because it is the most crooked street in America. No visit to San Francisco is complete without a ride on a cable car or a seafood repast at Fisherman's Wharf. Tourists will also want to stroll through the Japanese garden in Golden Gate Park or meander through the colorful shops of Chinatown.

San Francisco is a city of natural beauty and fascinating sites. Visitors will not want to miss

seeing the Golden Gate Bridge and Park, Lombard Street, eating at Fisherman's Wharf, visiting

Chinatown, or riding on a cable car.

San Francisco lies atop the San Andreas Fault, which extends hundreds of miles along the Pacific Coast. In 1906, the city was almost completely destroyed by an earthquake. The first shock occurred at 5:13 A.M., while most of the city was still asleep. Buildings toppled over, bringing down with them electric wires. Five minutes later, there was another shock, which ripped up pavements and streetcar tracks. Gas mains exploded, and water mains broke. A fire broke out and raged out of control for three days. Without water, firefighters had no way to put out the blaze. The disaster left more than 300,000 people homeless.

In 1906, San Francisco was almost completely destroyed by an earthquake and the destructive

fire that followed.

Skills Activity: Summarize a Paragraph, *Landscapes* **(Hardcover: pages 94-95)** *Enterprises* **(Softcover: pages 86-87)**
Objective: Summarize a paragraph *(Comprehension and Vocabulary Skills)*
Extension: Have students draw two lines under the supporting details for the main idea in each selection.

Name   Date

Read each paragraph. Then circle the letter of the best summary.

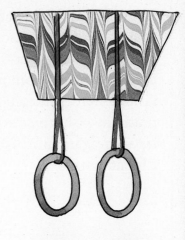

1.   Kurt Thomas began to study gymnastics when he was fourteen, and he continued the sport through college. He spent every day stretching, learning, and practicing on the bars, rings, pummel horse, and mats. His workouts were tough and painful; Kurt often spent twenty hours in one week practicing on the rings alone. Kurt's efforts eventually paid off, however, when he became a champion gymnast.

  a. Stretching, learning, and practicing are tough and painful.

  b. Kurt Thomas began gymnastics when he was fourteen.

  c. Kurt Thomas often spent twenty hours in one week on the rings.

  (d.) Hard work, determination, and practice have all contributed to Kurt Thomas' success as a gymnast.

2.   The movements in gymnastics are much more difficult than they look. To perform gymnastics, both the mind and the body must work together. The mind is needed to learn the skills and routines, and the body must be strong enough to perform them. A gymnast has to concentrate hard as he or she carries out every movement with strength, balance, and grace.

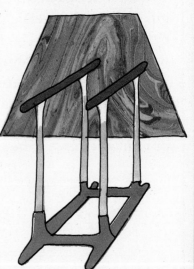

  (a.) The mind and the body of a gymnast must work together as he or she is performing.

  b. A person must be smart to learn the gymnastic skills and routines.

  c. A gymnast must be strong and graceful.

  d. Gymnastic skills are much more difficult than they look.

MACMILLAN PUBLISHING COMPANY

"Children's Express," *Landscapes* **(Hardcover: pages 96-104)** *Enterprises* **(Softcover: pages 88-96)**

Objective: Summarize a paragraph *(Comprehension and Vocabulary Skills)*

Extension: Have students write a paragraph about a favorite activity they do in gym class. Then have them write one sentence summarizing the paragraph.

Name _____   Date _____

A. Match each word in Column 1 with its definition in Column 2. Write the letter of the definition on the lines below.

Column 1	**Column 2**
___f___ **1.** attitude	**a.** provided with a goal
___d___ **2.** cultural	**b.** part of a sports performance
___g___ **3.** organization	**c.** a person who prepares material for publication
___a___ **4.** motivated	**d.** relating to a people's way of life
___c___ **5.** editor	**e.** to take part in
___e___ **6.** participate	**f.** a manner of thinking
___b___ **7.** routine	**g.** a group of people with one purpose

B. Read the sentences below. Then use the words from Column 1 above to complete each sentence.

1. The Children's Express news service is an ever-growing ___organization___.

2. A good news reporter must be ___motivated___ to go out and get a news story.

3. One exciting part of news reporting is the chance to ___participate___ in making the news.

4. The ___editor___ rewrote part of the reporter's story.

5. The ice skater's ___routine___ was vividly described in an article in the sports section.

6. The newspaper listed several ___cultural___ events that were to take place over the weekend.

7. A positive ___attitude___ is necessary in the tough job of reporting the news.

"**Children's Express,**" *Landscapes* (Hardcover: pages 96-104) *Enterprises* (Softcover: pages 88-96)

Objective: Use vocabulary words *(Comprehension and Vocabulary Skills)*

Extension: Have students write the base word of: *cultural, organization, motivated, editor.*

27

Name _____ Date _____

A. Below are some statements about "Children's Express." Write **T** if the statement is true. Write **F** if it is false.

_____T_____ **1.** Children's Express was founded by Robert Clampitt in 1975.

_____F_____ **2.** There are five kinds of Children's Express newspaper columns.

_____F_____ **3.** A briefing is a kind of interview.

_____T_____ **4.** The first Children's Express bureau was set up in Salem, Massachusetts.

_____F_____ **5.** Kurt Thomas is a swimmer who has competed in the Olympics.

_____T_____ **6.** Thomas believes that winning isn't the most important thing in sports.

_____T_____ **7.** Children's Express started as a magazine.

B. Use complete sentences to answer these questions about "Children's Express."
(Answers will vary.)

1. What do Children's Express reporters talk about in their roundtable discussions?

They discuss their feelings and experiences about a variety of topics, such as working mothers

or what makes a person heroic.

2. How did Children's Express get into newspapers?

A newspaper syndicate asked Robert Clampitt if Children's Express would create a column

for newspapers.

3. Why does Kurt Thomas think too much pressure isn't good for a young athlete?

He feels that the pressure takes the fun out of sports, makes failure unbearable, and turns

the athlete away from his or her sport.

4. What does Robert Clampitt see as the future of Children's Express?

He sees a worldwide network of bureaus linked by computers and providing a full cultural

exchange between countries.

MACMILLAN PUBLISHING COMPANY

"Children's Express," *Landscapes* **(Hardcover: pages 96-104)** *Enterprises* **(Softcover: pages 88-96)**
Objective: Demonstrate story comprehension *(Comprehension and Vocabulary Skills)*

Name _____ Date _____

Read the crossword puzzle clues. Then use the suffixes in the box to complete the puzzle.

| -ar | -er | -or | -ist | -an | -ian | -less | -ward |

ACROSS
1. one who draws cartoons
2. of or like an angle
3. one who invents
4. without sugar
5. one who reports
6. one who practices magic

DOWN
7. one who was born or lives in Mexico
8. one who plays the guitar
9. one who makes sculpture
10. one who is skilled in art
11. one who is skilled in music
12. toward the east

"Children's Express," *Landscapes* (Hardcover: pages 96-104) *Enterprises* (Softcover: pages 88-96)

Objective: Identify suffixes: *-ar, -er, -or, -ist, -an, -ian, -less, -ward* (*Decoding Skills and Phonics Skills*)

Extension: Have students write a paragraph using as many words from the page as possible.

29

Name _____ Date _____

Use context clues to choose the best meaning for the underlined word in each sentence. Fill in the circle next to your answer.

1. Spices such as cinnamon and cloves come from <u>aromatic</u>, or fragrant, plants that grow primarily in the tropics.
   - (a) flower bearing
   - (b) sweet smelling ●
   - (c) tropical
   - (d) sharp tasting

2. The <u>Moluccas</u> (the Spice Islands) are now a famous source of spices, but for centuries this source was a secret carefully guarded by Arabian traders.
   - (a) Sandwich Islands
   - (b) Asia
   - (c) Spice Islands ●
   - (d) Arabia

3. The Arabs' secret was <u>disclosed</u> in the thirteenth century; Marco Polo revealed it in his writings about his travels through Asia and China.
   - (a) not opened
   - (b) kept secret
   - (c) traveled
   - (d) made known ●

4. Spices were first used to improve the flavor of food that was <u>tainted</u>. Now, of course, people simply don't eat food that has spoiled.
   - (a) going bad ●
   - (b) plain tasting
   - (c) delicious
   - (d) unappealing

5. Spices improve either the taste or the smell of foods. While they provide no <u>nutrition</u>, they do make one feel hungrier and help with digestion.
   - (a) value as food ●
   - (b) smell
   - (c) vitamins
   - (d) taste

6. It was in search of spices that Christopher Columbus ventured forth into <u>uncharted</u> waters. Instead of finding the Spice Islands, he discovered the New World.
   - (a) unexplored ●
   - (b) stormy
   - (c) not shallow
   - (d) unsafe for small ships

7. During World War II, many East Indian sources of spice were destroyed. Thus, the pepper supply in the United States <u>dwindled</u>.
   - (a) divided
   - (b) supplied
   - (c) decreased ●
   - (d) increased

"Mysteriously Yours, Maggie Marmelstein," *Landscapes* **(Hardcover: pages 108-121)** *Enterprises* **(Softcover: pages 100-113)**

Objective: Define words using context clues *(Comprehension and Vocabulary Skills)*

Extension: Have students look up and write a sentence containing context clues for each of the following words: *emerge, placid, prod, query, wisp.*

Name _____   Date _____

A. Read the definitions below. Then match each definition in the box by finding and circling the word in the word puzzle below. The words are printed across, down, diagonal, and backwards.

survey	intriguing	qualifications
consultant	inspired	approximately

1. abilities that make a person fit for a certain job
2. a person who gives professional advice
3. a detailed study or investigation
4. nearly correct or exact
5. arousing the curiosity of
6. stimulated; stirred

```
a  d  g  n  o  p  i  q  r  s  t  u  l  u
b  e  l  m  b  i  n  s  p  i  r  e  d  m
c  f  j  t  n  a  t  l  u  s  n  o  c  p
h  i  k  a  c  d  r  z  y  x  w  v  o  n
q  u  a  l  i  f  i  c  a  t  i  o  n  s
j  i  h  g  f  e  g  q  t  u  v  w  x  y
k  l  m  n  o  p  u  r  s  d  c  y  b  z
a  p  p  r  o  x  i  m  a  t  e  l  y  a
a  w  x  t  u  v  n  e  f  v  g  h  i  j
b  z  y  s  r  q  g  p  r  o  n  l  m  k
h  c  d  e  f  g  b  u  i  j  k  l  p  q
z  y  q  v  w  x  s  r  s  t  u  a  c  g
```

B. Read the story below. Then use the words in the box above to complete the sentences.

Jonathan was _____ inspired _____ to join the school paper after hearing a professional journalist speak to his class. His first assignment for the paper was to take a _____ survey _____ of how students felt on important issues. The results were certainly _____ intriguing _____ and not at all what the paper's staff expected. Jonathan reported his findings, stating that _____ approximately _____ 75% of the fifth graders at Roosevelt School watched the news nightly. When Tina read this, she believed that she and her classmates had the necessary _____ qualifications _____ to organize a _____ consultant _____ team to advise and help the Debating Club research current issues.

"**Mysteriously Yours, Maggie Marmelstein,**" *Landscapes* (Hardcover: pages 108-121) *Enterprises* (Softcover: pages 100-113)

Objective: Use vocabulary words *(Comprehension and Vocabulary Skills)*

Extension: Have students write three sentences using the following word pairs: *inspired, qualifications; approximately, survey; intriguing, consultant.*

Name _____   Date _____

A. Match the characters from "Mysteriously Yours, Maggie Marmelstein" by writing the letter of the phrase that describes each character below.

_e_ **1.** Mrs. Marmelstein

_d_ **2.** Maggie

_a_ **3.** Noah

_c_ **4.** Thad

_b_ **5.** Ellen

a. came up with an intriguing way to promote the school paper

b. was hard to get to know

c. wasn't interested in the paper until the Mystery Person contest

d. was chosen to be the Mystery Person

e. became the Mystery Person's consultant

B. Use complete sentences to answer these questions about "Mysteriously Yours, Maggie Marmelstein." (Answers will vary.)

1. What two qualities did Noah think the Mystery Person should have?

He thought the Mystery Person should be a good writer and a good keeper of secrets.

2. What clue in the notice told Maggie that she was to be the Mystery Person?

The word flavor was used twice. This was the same word that Maggie used in describing

her entry to Noah.

3. Why do you think Maggie felt she would give herself away if she wrote about Cary Grant in her first column?

Maggie's friends knew that she was a big fan of

Cary Grant.

4. Do you think you would like to be the Mystery Person in this story? Why or why not?

"Mysteriously Yours, Maggie Marmelstein," *Landscapes* (Hardcover: pages 108-121) *Enterprises* (Softcover: pages 100-113)

Objective: Demonstrate story comprehension *(Comprehension and Vocabulary Skills)*

32

Name _____ Date _____

A. Read each sentence. Decide which phrase below might replace the underlined words. Circle the letter next to your answer.

1. The reporter just couldn't stay tough when faced by the angry mayor in an interview.
   - **a.** took a chance
   - **(b.)** lost his nerve
   - **c.** faced the music
   - **d.** walked a tightrope

2. The surface of the frozen pond was perfectly smooth.
   - **(a.)** like a polished mirror
   - **b.** like a dark night
   - **c.** like a velvet carpet
   - **d.** like a razor's edge

3. Maggie was exhausted after writing half the night.
   - **a.** so happy she could jump for joy
   - **b.** so wild she should have been in the zoo
   - **c.** so lazy she couldn't even tie her shoelace
   - **(d.)** so tired she could have slept for a week

4. Suddenly, the rainspout was pouring forth huge amounts of water.
   - **a.** a raging blizzard
   - **b.** a lost raindrop
   - **(c.)** a gushing waterfall
   - **d.** a leaky faucet

B. Each sentence below contains a figure of speech. If the figure of speech is a metaphor, write **M**. If it is a simile, write **S**. If it is an idiom, write **I**. If it is an example of hyperbole, write **H**.

_S_ **1.** The snow was blown about as wildly as popping corn.

_H_ **2.** I was so greedy for knowledge that I could have read every book in the library.

_I_ **3.** Our school paper missed the boat on that news story.

_M_ **4.** The fog was a thick curtain of gray.

_S_ **5.** The presses roared like ferocious beasts.

_I_ **6.** After winning the writing contest, I was walking on air for the rest of the week.

_I_ **7.** When Maggie won the Mystery Person contest, her lips were sealed.

_M_ **8.** Judy was a busy bee doing her chores all day.

"Mysteriously Yours, Maggie Marmelstein," *Landscapes* (Hardcover: pages 108-121) *Enterprises* (Softcover: pages 100-113)

Objective: Interpret figurative language: simile, metaphor, idiom, hyperbole *(Literature and Language Skills)*

Extension: Have students choose and illustrate one of the sentences containing figurative language from Part B.

33

Name _____ Date _____

Read the definitions below. Then fill in the circle next to the word that is defined.

1. a person who prepares written material
   - (a) edit
   - (b) devices
   - (c) profit
   - **(d) editor**

2. knowledge making a person fit for a certain job
   - (a) publish
   - **(b) qualifications**
   - (c) chore
   - (d) employer

3. arousing the curiosity of; fascinating
   - **(a) intriguing**
   - (b) attitude
   - (c) motivated
   - (d) participate

4. to produce printed material
   - (a) publicity
   - (b) routine
   - **(c) publish**
   - (d) edit

5. nearly exact or correct
   - (a) profit
   - (b) investments
   - (c) enterprise
   - **(d) approximately**

6. a detailed study
   - **(a) survey**
   - (b) slogan
   - (c) rate
   - (d) consumer

7. a prepared talk on a subject
   - (a) negotiating
   - (b) permit
   - **(c) lecture**
   - (d) recommendation

8. a manner of thinking or feeling
   - (a) motivated
   - **(b) attitude**
   - (c) cultural
   - (d) participate

9. not clearly expressed
   - (a) edit
   - (b) publicity
   - (c) journal
   - **(d) vague**

10. a person who gives professional advice
    - (a) profession
    - (b) market
    - **(c) consultant**
    - (d) interview

11. the ability to take a first step in doing something
    - (a) interview
    - (b) investments
    - (c) profession
    - **(d) initiative**

12. the act of speaking favorably about someone or something
    - **(a) recommendation**
    - (b) enterprise
    - (c) publicity
    - (d) interview

13. bringing about or arranging the terms of an agreement
    - (a) investments
    - (b) profit
    - **(c) negotiating**
    - (d) publicity

14. provided with a goal that causes a person to act
    - (a) cultural
    - (b) participate
    - (c) enterprise
    - **(d) motivated**

15. a difficult or important project
    - (a) slogan
    - **(b) enterprise**
    - (c) participate
    - (d) publicity

Cumulative Vocabulary Review

Objective: Use vocabulary words (Comprehension and Vocabulary Skills)

Extension: Have students choose five words from the page and write a sentence for each word.

34

Name _____ Date _____

A. Read each pair of sentences. Then write **C** next to the sentence that states the cause and **E** next to the sentence that states the effect.

__C__ **1.** The newscaster predicted showers in the afternoon.

__E__ **2.** Joyce wore her slicker and took an umbrella to school.

__E__ **1.** Kristen registered for a photography class.

__C__ **2.** Kristen enjoys photography.

__E__ **1.** Peter collected newspapers, bottles, and cans.

__C__ **2.** Peter's class had set up a collection center for recycling certain materials.

B. Read the paragraph. Then complete the chart by supplying the missing cause or effect.

Since several families were planning to journey west, they met at the town hall to make the final arrangements. The Mitchells volunteered to arrange for oxen, horses, and mules to pull the heavy wagons because they had the largest farm and the most animals. Everyone agreed to take very little furniture because they had heard that heavy wagons had to be emptied along the way.

CAUSE	EFFECT
Several families planned to journey west.	They met in the town hall to make the final arrangements.
They had the largest farm and the most animals.	The Mitchells volunteered to arrange for oxen, horses, and mules to pull the heavy wagons.
They had heard that heavy wagons had to be emptied along the way.	Everyone agreed to take very little furniture.

"Diablo Blanco," *Landscapes* (Hardcover: pages 146-159) *Frontiers* (Softcover: pages 10-23)

Objective: Identify cause-and-effect relationships: stated or implied *(Comprehension and Vocabulary Skills)*

Extension: Have students rewrite the sentences in Part A, using signal words to combine each cause and effect into a single sentence.

Name   Date

A. Match each word with its definition. Write the letter of the word on the line next to its definition below.

a. excelled   __d__ to manage cleverly

b. determined   __e__ lasting forever

c. pursuit   __a__ became better in ability or skill

d. maneuver   __f__ the greatest in importance

e. eternal   __b__ having a fixed purpose

f. principal   __c__ the act of following in order to overtake

B. Read the following sentences. Put a ✔ next to each sentence in which the underlined word is used incorrectly.

_____ **1.** The principal speaker for the program was seated at the head of the table.

✔ **2.** John excelled at mathematics since he couldn't understand how to add or subtract.

_____ **3.** He was determined to learn how to ice skate.

✔ **4.** He was principal in the basketball tournament.

✔ **5.** The rain was eternal as soon as the sun came out.

_____ **6.** Sharon had to maneuver her way through the crowded entrance.

✔ **7.** Paul had to pursuit in order to score a goal for his team.

_____ **8.** Jannette was the best guitarist in her class; she excelled at playing the guitar.

_____ **9.** The soldiers were honored by an eternal flame that burned in Veteran Park.

_____ **10.** Barbara was in pursuit of her lost puppy all morning.

"Diablo Blanco," *Landscapes* (Hardcover: pages 146-159) *Frontiers* (Softcover: pages 10-23)

Objective: Use vocabulary words *(Comprehension and Vocabulary Skills)*

Extension: Have students use the dictionary to find other meanings for the word *principal*.

36

Name   Date

A. Match each sentence beginning with an ending that will make a true statement about "Diablo Blanco." Write the letter of the ending on the line.

_____c_____ **1.** Roberto's grandfather

_____a_____ **2.** Roberto's father

_____e_____ **3.** Yellow Cloud told Roberto that he

_____b_____ **4.** Roberto learned that the wild horses

_____d_____ **5.** Robert told Chief Leaning Rock that he

a. had been killed trying to capture Diablo Blanco.

b. ran in great circles.

c. had saved Chief Leaning Rock's life.

d. wanted to learn horsemanship.

e. could become a Comanche.

B. Write complete sentences to answer the following questions about "Diablo Blanco." (Answers will vary.)

1. Why do you think Roberto wanted to go to Conas before he made an attempt to capture Diablo Blanco?

Roberto knew he had to become an expert horseman before he could capture Diablo Blanco.

2. Why did Roberto capture several other horses before he began his pursuit of Diablo Blanco?

Roberto needed one horse to trade for supplies and two other horses to use in his pursuit

of Diablo.

3. Why didn't Roberto keep Cactus and sell his Comanche horse?

Roberto kept the Comanche horse because it was trained to help capture mustangs. Therefore,

the Comanche horse was more valuable to Roberto than Cactus.

4. How did Roberto's knowledge of the habits of mustangs help him capture Diablo Blanco?

Because he had learned that mustangs ran in circles, he knew where to locate his camp and

how to relay horses.

"Diablo Blanco," *Landscapes* **(Hardcover: pages 146-159)** *Frontiers* **(Softcover: pages 10-23)**

Objective: Demonstrate story comprehension *(Comprehension and Vocabulary Skills)*

Name   Date

Use the encyclopedia set to answer the question below. Circle the letter next to the best answer. Some questions will have more than one answer.

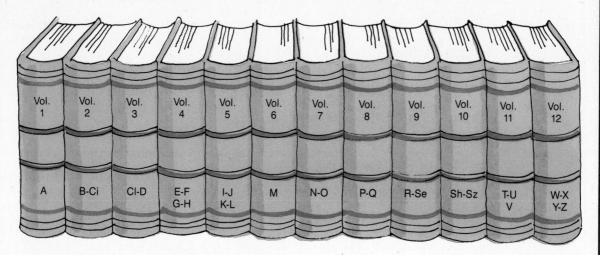

Vol. 1	Vol. 2	Vol. 3	Vol. 4	Vol. 5	Vol. 6	Vol. 7	Vol. 8	Vol. 9	Vol. 10	Vol. 11	Vol. 12
A	B-Ci	Cl-D	E-F G-H	I-J K-L	M	N-O	P-Q	R-Se	Sh-Sz	T-U V	W-X Y-Z

1. In which volume would you look to find information about wild horses on the western frontier?

   a. 4   **b.** 5   **c.** 11   **d.** 12

2. Which key word should you use to find the answer to the question below? What were the highlights of President Thomas Jefferson's administration?

   a. President   **b.** Jefferson   **c.** Thomas   **d.** administration

3. Between which two guide words would you expect to find information about the explorer Hernando Cortés?

   a. Coronado/cortisone   **b.** hermit crab/heron

   c. cosmos/cougar   **d.** exodus/extensor

4. In which volume would you find information about the Comanches?

   a. 4   **b.** 7   **c.** 3   **d.** 8

5. Which key word or words could you use to find information to answer the question below?

   In what part of Mexico was the Aztec empire located?

   a. empire   **b.** Mexico   **c.** Aztec   **d.** location

6. Between which two guide words would you expect to find information about lava?

   a. Laurier/Laver, Rod   **b.** Latium/Latvia

   c. Launching/Laurel   **d.** Laval/Lavender

"Diablo Blanco," *Landscapes* (Hardcover: pages 146-159) *Frontiers* (Softcover: pages 10-23)

Objective: Use reference sources: encyclopedia, almanac, atlas *(Study Skills)*

Extension: Have students write the volume number for the answers chosen for questions 2, 3, 5, and 6.

38

MACMILLAN PUBLISHING COMPANY

Name   Date

This map shows the major trails taken by the men and
women who left the East to travel westward. Study the map.
Then answer the questions below.

PIONEER ROADS AND TRAILS

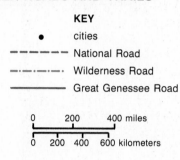

KEY
- • cities
- – – – – National Road
- – · – · – · Wilderness Road
- ——— Great Genessee Road

0   200   400 miles

0   200   400   600 kilometers

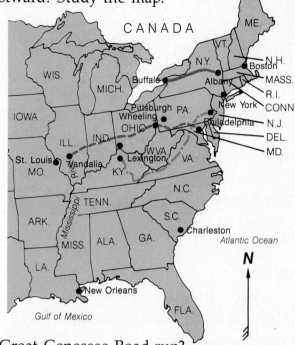

1. In what general direction does the Great Genessee Road run?

   East-West

2. Which two cities are connected by the Great Genessee Road?

   Buffalo and Albany

3. Which road runs from Philadelphia, Pennsylvania, to Lexington, Kentucky?

   Wilderness Road

4. What is the westernmost city on the National Road?

   Vandalia

5. Of the trails shown, which two are about equal in length?

   National Road and Wilderness Road

6. In what state does the National Road cross the Wilderness Road?

   Maryland

7. About how many miles long is the Great Genessee Road?

   about 250 miles long

"Going West," *Landscapes* **(Hardcover: pages 160-169)** *Frontiers* **(Softcover: pages 24-33)**

Objective: Interpret graphic aids: maps (key, north arrow, scale bar)
(Study Skills)

Extension: Have students use the map scale to find the distance in miles
of the Wilderness Road and the National Road.

Name _____ Date _____

A. Read the clues. Then use words from the box to complete the crossword puzzle.

typical	abandoned	fatigue
fertile	emigrant	frontier

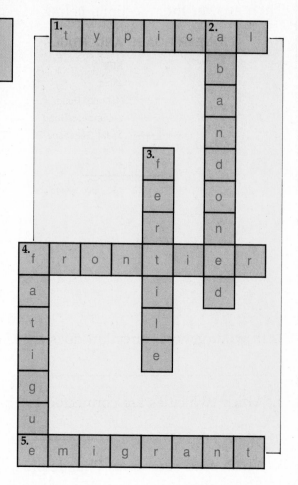

ACROSS

1. regular; ordinary; usual
4. border between settled and unsettled territory
5. a person who leaves one place or country to live in another

DOWN

2. left behind or alone; deserted
3. producing or able to produce crops abundantly
4. exhaustion

___

B. Use words from the box above to complete these sentences.

1. In his letter, the pioneer boy described a _____typical_____ day on a prairie farm.

2. After working from sunrise to sunset, the farmer's _____fatigue_____ showed on his face.

3. Although few trees grew on the prairie, the land was _____fertile_____ enough for growing corn and wheat.

4. The town eventually became a "ghost" town; everyone had _____abandoned_____ it.

5. Pioneers helped push the American _____frontier_____ farther and farther west.

"Going West," *Landscapes* (Hardcover: pages 160-169) *Frontiers* (Softcover: pages 24-33)

Objective: Use vocabulary words *(Comprehension and Vocabulary Skills)*

Extension: Have students write a paragraph using the words in the box in Part A.

40

Name   Date

A. Read the following statements. If the statement is true, write **T**. If the statement is false, write **F**. Then rewrite the false statements to make them true. (Sentences will vary.)

_____F_____ **1.** Pioneers traveled in small groups because it was safer.

It was safer to travel in large groups.

_____T_____ **2.** It was not unusual to find grave markers beside the Oregon Trail.

_____F_____ **3.** After the continental divide, travel was easier.

There were still high mountains to be crossed.

_____F_____ **4.** At that time, California was a part of the United States.

California was then part of Mexico.

_____F_____ **5.** It did not matter when a wagon party started its journey west.

It was critical to start out in mid-spring.

B. Use complete sentences to answer the following questions about "Going West." (Answers will vary.)

1. In what state did the Oregon Trail begin?

It began in Missouri.

2. What were some of the things the average wagon contained?

The wagon was crammed with the family's possessions—food, clothing, furniture, tools,

bedding, kitchenware, and tent supplies.

3. What happened when the train captain gave the signal to stop for the night?

The wagons pulled off the trail and formed a large circle.

4. Why were the early pioneers headed for the Pacific Coast?

They went to claim free land in Oregon and California territories or to strike it rich by mining

gold and silver.

"Going West," *Landscapes* (Hardcover: pages 160-169) *Frontiers* (Softcover: pages 24-33)

Objective: Demonstrate story comprehension *(Comprehension and Vocabulary Skills)*

Name _____   Date _____

Read each passage below. Then choose one or more phrases from the box to answer each question. Write your choice on the lines below.

PURPOSE	POINT OF VIEW
to entertain the reader	angry and exasperated
to inform the reader	sad but hopeful
to record events	happy and cheerful

                                        May 1, 1842

Dear Diary,

   We're on our way! Pa says we'll follow the Oregon Trail and settle in Oregon Territory. Pa is going to build a house for us. We'll have our own land to farm. Sean wants to raise goats, and I want some rabbits. Our wagons are filled with food, supplies, and furniture. Ma is worried that we won't make it. But when Pa smiles at her, she stops worrying and smiles, too. I'll talk to you tomorrow, Diary.

                                        Keri

What is the author's purpose? to record events _____

What is the author's point of view or feelings? happy and cheerful _____

                                        December 24, 1842

Dear Sarah,

   It's Christmas Eve. We've been traveling for almost eight months. Sean keeps asking me to tell him what Christmas was like last year. Every time I get to the part about the turkey dinner Ma and I fixed, I begin to cry. Our wagons are empty. We had to throw all our belongings out when we crossed the Rocky Mountains. The wagons were just too heavy for the oxen and mules. We have no food left. We're so hungry and so cold. Pa says we won't be traveling much longer. Soon...Soon...I guess maybe tomorrow. I miss you.

                                        Your cousin, Keri

What is the author's purpose? to inform the reader _____

What is the author's point of view or feelings? sad but hopeful _____

"Going West," *Landscapes* **(Hardcover: pages 160-169)** *Frontiers* **(Softcover: pages 24-33)**

Objective: Identify author's purpose and point of view (*Comprehension and Vocabulary Skills*)

Extension: Have students choose a purpose and point of view from the box on this page and write a pioneer's diary entry of their own.

42

Name   Date

Use the map and its key to answer the questions. Fill in the circle next to the answers below.

Highways of the West

1. In what direction does Interstate Highway 80 run?
   (a) north/south   (b) east/west   (c) northeast   (d) southwest

2. In what state does Interstate Highway 80 branch off into 80N?
   (a) Utah   (b) Idaho   (c) California   (d) Wyoming

3. Which of the following highways run through Texas?
   (a) 35, 10, 30, 5   (b) 20, 80, 70, 90   (c) 10, 35, 20, 25   (d) 25, 82, 35, 10

4. In what direction do Interstate Highways 35 and 15 run?
   (a) north/south   (b) east/west   (c) northeast   (d) southwest

5. Which of the following highways ends in Oklahoma?
   (a) 40   (b) 35   (c) 30   (d) 44

6. In what state do Interstate Highways 70 and 25 intersect?
   (a) Wyoming   (b) New Mexico   (c) Colorado   (d) Kansas

"Going West," *Landscapes* (Hardcover: pages 160-169) *Frontiers* (Softcover: pages 24-33)

Objective: Interpret graphic aids: maps (key, north arrow, scale bar) *(Study Skills)*

Extension: Have students write the directions for a journey from the Mississippi River to Sacramento, California.

Name _____   Date _____

Read the paragraph. Then fill in the circle before the phrase that correctly completes each statement below.

Because there were few trees on the prairies, the settlers built their first homes from sod. It took about an acre of prairie to provide enough sod for a small, one-room house. Each sod "brick" weighed about fifty pounds. The bricks would be stacked one on top of the other to form the four walls of the house. Holes would, of course, be left for doors and windows. The roof was made of brush, or shrubs and bushes, with a final layer of sod which was supported by a crisscross of willows. Because its walls were so thick, the inside of the house was cool in summer and warm during the cold, prairie winter. The house protected the family from wind and fire, but not from rain. Long after a rainfall, water would drip from the roof. In dry spells, pieces of dirt would fall. To help catch the dirt, some settlers lined the roof with cheesecloth. Because the houses were made from sod, they were called "soddies," and the pioneers who built them became known as "sodbusters." Later, when they could afford to import lumber from other areas, many families replaced their soddies with frame houses.

1. The prairie settlers built homes from sod because _____.
   - (a) soddies were windproof
   - (b) wood was not fireproof
   - **(c) lumber was scarce**
   - (d) they were sodbusters

2. Because of the materials they used to build their first homes, prairie settlers were called _____.
   - (a) squatters
   - **(b) sodbusters**
   - (c) bricklayers
   - (d) soddies

3. The roof of a sod house was sometimes lined with cheesecloth in order to _____.
   - (a) support the sod
   - (b) keep out the rain
   - (c) provide decoration
   - **(d) catch falling dirt**

4. Because it was built with thick bricks of earth, the sod house _____.
   - (a) had plastered walls
   - (b) felt cool in winter
   - (c) had no windows
   - **(d) felt cool in summer**

"By the Shores of Silver Lake," *Landscapes* (Hardcover: pages 174-188) *Frontiers* (Softcover: pages 38-52)

Objective: Identify cause-and-effect relationships: stated or implied (*Comprehension and Vocabulary Skills*)

Extension: Have students write the four sentences on this page, and label the cause and effect in each.

MACMILLAN PUBLISHING COMPANY

Name _____ Date _____

A. Match each word in the box with its definition. Write the word one letter to a line. The name of the main character in "By the Shores of Silver Lake" will appear in the puzzle box.

| vacant | persuasion | shelter | file | boarders |

1. to hand in officially
2. empty or unoccupied
3. the act of convincing someone of something
4. thing that protects from weather or danger
5. persons who pay for meals and lodging

1.   f   i   l   e

2.   v   a   c   a   n   t

3.   p   e   r   s   u   a   s   i   o   n

4. s   h   e   l   t   e   r

5.   b   o   a   r   d   e   r   s

B. Use each pair of words in a sentence on the lines below. (Sentences will vary.)

1. **vacant/shelter** _____

_____

_____

2. **boarders/persuasion** _____

_____

_____

3. **file/vacant** _____

_____

_____

"**By the Shores of Silver Lake,**" *Landscapes* (Hardcover: pages 174-188) *Frontiers* (Softcover: pages 38-52)

Objective: Use vocabulary words *(Comprehension and Vocabulary Skills)*

Extension: Have students use a dictionary to write sentences showing other meanings of the word *file* and identifying whether they used it as a noun or a verb.

Name   Date

A. Use a complete sentence to answer the following questions about "By the Shores of Silver Lake." (Answers will vary.)

1. What did Pa think would happen to the greenhorns if they tried to get to Huron at night?

He thought they'd lose their way on the prairie and maybe freeze to death.

2. Why did it take Pa so long to file his homestead claim?

When Pa showed up at the Land Office, he couldn't get near the door because there were

so many people. He had to camp out there overnight.

3. How did Laura know that it had been Mr. Edwards who had helped Pa at the Land Office?

She knew because Pa described the way he yelled, and Laura had heard him yell like that

in Indian territory.

4. Why didn't Mr. Edwards want to come home with Pa?

He wanted to stay and protect his claim from claim jumpers.

5. Why did Pa refer to his claim as a "bet"?

Pa called it a bet because if he stayed on the land for five years, he could keep it. Otherwise,

he would lose it.

B. Place a check next to the adjectives that could describe Pa. Then briefly describe each checked adjective with an event from the story. (Sentences will vary.)

_____ regretful   ✔ persistent   _____ fearsome

✔ hard-working   ✔ friendly   _____ stingy

hard-working   Pa shows this trait in building a store.

persistent   This trait is shown in Pa's waiting all night on line at the Land Office to file his claim.

friendly   This trait is shown in his welcome to greenhorns who were on their way to Huron.

MACMILLAN PUBLISHING COMPANY

"By the Shores of Silver Lake," *Landscapes* **(Hardcover: pages 174-188)** *Frontiers* **(Softcover: pages 38-52)**

Objective: Demonstrate story comprehension *(Comprehension and Vocabulary Skills)*

Name   Date

A. Add the prefix to the base word to form a new word. Then write the definition of the new word.

Prefix	Base Word	New Word	Definition
1. re-	gain	regain	to get back, or gain again
2. re-	arrange	rearrange	to arrange again
3. dis-	honest	dishonest	not honest
4. dis-	agree	disagree	the opposite of agree
5. ir-	relevant	irrelevant	not relevant
6. im-	measurable	immeasurable	not able to be measured
7. in-	accurate	inaccurate	not accurate
8. in-	active	inactive	not active
9. il-	legible	illegible	not legible

B. Use the new words you formed in Exercise A to complete the following sentences.

1. Helping the younger children learn to read gave Susan _____immeasurable_____ satisfaction.

2. Our answers to the math problems do not agree; could your answers be _____inaccurate_____?

3. Many of his remarks were _____irrelevant_____ to the conversation.

4. Our team lost the championship game this year, but we hope to _____regain_____ the title next year.

5. Let's _____rearrange_____ our desks so that we sit in alphabetical order.

6. An _____inactive_____ person should eat less than one who gets a lot of exercise.

7. Mary and Carrie often _____disagree_____, but they are still the best of friends.

"**By the Shores of Silver Lake,**" *Landscapes* (Hardcover: pages 174-188) *Frontiers* (Softcover: pages 38-52)

Objective: Identify prefixes: *re-, dis-, im-, in-, il-, ir-* (Decoding and Phonics Skills)

Extension: Have students write other words with the prefixes *re-, dis-, im-, in-, il-,* and *ir-* and use them in sentences of their own.

Name _____ Date _____

Read the passage. Then circle the letter next to the generalization that can be drawn from it.

The year was 1874; the season, summer. Grasshoppers, millions of them, swarmed onto the Great Plains. They stripped the trees bare and destroyed millions of acres of wheat and corn. Grasshoppers even stalled trains. The crushed bodies of the insects made the tracks so slippery that the locomotive's wheels spun helplessly on the tracks. Grasshoppers invaded dry-goods stores, devouring any cloth that had starch in it. Regardless of family members who attacked them with brooms, mops, and dustpans, the grasshoppers invaded homes. They got into food, milk, water, and anything that was not tightly sealed. There were so many grasshoppers that people couldn't even raise the cover of a pan on the stove without grasshoppers jumping in. They even crawled down the spouts of tea kettles! Farmers were pleased that the grasshoppers provided food for their chickens. However, the chickens ate too many and died. In desperation, settlers used fire and smoke to destroy these insects, but nothing could stop the plague. Millions of grasshoppers swept across North Dakota, South Dakota, Nebraska, Kansas, Oklahoma, Wyoming, and Colorado every summer from 1874 through 1877.

a. During the 1870s, grasshoppers were a nuisance to all who tried to farm on the Great Plains.

b. During the 1870s, grasshoppers caused trouble throughout the United States.

c. During the 1870s, grasshoppers stalled trains, ate crops, and killed chickens.

(d.) During the 1870s, millions of grasshoppers were responsible for much trouble and destruction on the Great Plains.

"By the Shores of Silver Lake," *Landscapes* (Hardcover: pages 174-188) *Frontiers* (Softcover: pages 38-52)

Objective: Make generalizations *(Comprehension and Vocabulary Skills)*

Extension: Have students underline the clues that helped them choose the generalization on this page.

MACMILLAN PUBLISHING COMPANY

Name _____   Date _____

Read each paragraph. Then fill in the circle before the phrase that best completes each statement.

Landscape painting was popular in Europe long before American artists began landscape painting. Most European artists painted peaceful scenes, often of life in rustic villages or in the countryside. American landscape artists were in awe of the untamed beauty of America. Albert Bierstadt's huge canvases reflect the majesty of the Rocky Mountains. Other artists who painted in the East painted equally romantic pictures of the land. Albert Bierstadt worked with a group of artists who came to be known as the Hudson River School. This group of artists helped to develop a strictly American style of landscape painting.

1. The author probably wrote this passage to _____.
- (a) explain how to create a landscape painting
- **(b) describe the early American style of landscape painting**
- (c) entertain with a story of high adventure
- (d) persuade others to study landscape painting

One of the first things an art student must learn is how to prepare a palette for oil painting. First, a generous amount of white paint is squeezed out onto the corner of the palette above the thumb hole. Other colors are then placed along the outside edge of the palette. The lighter shades such as the yellows and ochres are placed closest to the white. Then little bits of various shades of red are placed around the outside of the palette, ending with the darkest shade of blue. This leaves a large area in the center of the palette for color mixing.

2. The author seems to feel that _____.
- **(a) there is one best way to prepare an oil painter's palette**
- (b) mixing colors may result in a muddy-looking painting
- (c) white is the most important color for an oil painter
- (d) paints on a palette should be in random order

"The Art of the Old West," *Landscapes* (Hardcover: pages 192-199) *Frontiers* (Softcover: pages 56-63)

Objective: Identify author's purpose and point of view
(Comprehension and Vocabulary Skills)

Extension: Have students write paragraphs with the purpose of persuading their readers to do something, such as visit a museum.

Name _____ Date _____

A. Use words from the box to finish the selection. Write one word on each blank line.

expeditions	exhibited	portraits	emphasize	sculpture	profile

Several of the pioneers who made _____ expeditions _____ into the western wilderness were artists. These talented people captured the West through their different styles of art. Some of the artists painted _____ portraits _____ of the Western Indians. Other artists created paintings of the western landscapes; many of these works _____ emphasize _____ the spaciousness of the land and the vastness of the mountains. Other pioneer artists preferred to work in _____ sculpture _____. One sculptor designed a coin. On one side of the coin was the _____ profile _____ of an Indian's head. Some of these paintings and sculptures are now _____ exhibited _____ in museums and have helped show what the early West was like.

B. On the lines below, write a definition of each word as it is used in the paragraph in Part A. (Answers will vary.)

1. expeditions   journeys made for a specific purpose
_____

2. portraits   paintings of a person
_____

3. emphasize   to stress
_____

4. sculpture   a type of art done by carving in stone or casting in metal
_____

5. profile   a side view of a face
_____

6. exhibited   put on public display
_____

"The Art of the Old West," *Landscapes* (Hardcover: pages 192-199) *Frontiers* (Softcover: pages 56-63)

Objective: Use vocabulary words *(Comprehension and Vocabulary Skills)*

Extension: Have students write a sentence for the following word pairs: *expeditions, sculpture; portraits, exhibited; profile, emphasize.*

50

Name _____   Date _____

Read the sentences. Then match one of the artists from "The Art of the Old West" in the box with the sentences by writing the artist's name on the lines below.

| George Catlin | Frederic Remington | Albert Bierstadt |
| James Earle Fraser | Charles Marion Russell | |

_____Frederic Remington_____ painted pictures that reflected the hardships of the Old West where settlers fought to establish new homes while Indians tried to protect their lands. Then later in life he turned to sculpture in order to give a fuller expression to action than was possible on a flat surface.

_____Charles Marion Russell_____ painted scenes which reflected his love of the open ranges, the Indian ways, the great sky, the wildlife, and the freedom of the West.

_____Albert Bierstadt_____ traveled the Oregon Trail and made sketches of the landscape, the early travelers, and their wagons.

_____James Earle Fraser_____ designed the famous five-cent coin known as the "Buffalo Nickel."

_____George Catlin_____ was a self-taught painter who decided to paint the Indians in their home land before the settlers reached them and changed their ways.

"The Art of the Old West," *Landscapes* (Hardcover: pages 192-199) *Frontiers* (Softcover: pages 56-63)

Objective: Demonstrate story comprehension *(Comprehension and Vocabulary Skills)*

Name _____ Date _____

Write a generalization that is supported by the information in each paragraph below. (Answers will vary, but sample answers are given.)

1. Willa Cather was an American novelist who was born in Virginia. In 1883, she moved to Nebraska with her family. She loved the prairies and the people who lived there. She especially loved to hear stories about the pioneers. In 1913, her novel *O Pioneers!* was published. It describes the lives of the early settlers. *My Ántonia*, another novel, is also about the hardships and the joys of pioneer life. Many of Willa Cather's short stories tell about those who went west in frontier times.

Willa Cather was a writer who wrote novels and short stories about the pioneers who went

west in frontier times.

_____

_____

2. Pierre Remington served as an officer in the cavalry, or military unit on horseback. He wrote special feature stories about horses for the newspaper. His son Frederic was fascinated by the stories. Father and son often attended fairs and races to see horses in competition. Some of Frederic's earliest paintings included soldiers on horseback. Frederic Remington asked that the following words be put on his grave: "He knew the horse."

Frederic Remington was very interested in horses throughout his life.

_____

_____

_____

"The Art of the Old West," *Landscapes* **(Hardcover: pages 192-199)** *Frontiers* **(Softcover: pages 56-63)**

Objective: Make generalizations *(Comprehension and Vocabulary Skills)*

Extension: Have students write a sentence stating a generalization about pioneers, wagon trains, and artists of the Old West.

Name _____   Date _____

A. Circle the letter of the word that best completes each sentence.

1. The _____ difference between sculpture and painting is that sculpture has three dimensions and paintings have two.
    (a.) principal   **b.** pursuit   **c.** fertile   **d.** eternal

2. A pioneer who left the borders of the United States called himself or herself a(n) _____.
    a. profile   **b.** maneuver   **(c.)** emigrant   **d.** frontier

3. Although it was badly battered, the covered wagon still provided its owners with some degree of _____.
    a. sculpture   **b.** vacant   **c.** boarder   **(d.)** shelter

4. There are _____ of several early American Presidents on display at the museum.
    a. expeditions   **b.** boarders   **(c.)** portraits   **d.** pursuits

5. In his later years, Frederic Remington _____ painting and turned to sculpture.
    a. exhibited   **(b.)** abandoned   **c.** determined   **d.** excelled

6. The pioneers were a hard-working and _____ group of people.
    a. fatigue   **b.** typical   **(c.)** determined   **d.** persuasion

---

B. Read the sentences below. Place a check on the line next to each sentence that uses the underlined word correctly.

✔ _____ 1. We were sure Ellen would win the swimming race since she <u>excelled</u> at the sport.

_____ 2. We walked slowly in <u>pursuit</u> of the ten children who followed us.

_____ 3. This good weather must be <u>eternal</u> since it looks like rain.

✔ _____ 4. The <u>fertile</u> ground produced a good corn crop this year.

_____ 5. The <u>typical</u> painting was unlike anything I had ever seen.

✔ _____ 6. The dog panted with <u>fatigue</u> after chasing a cat up the tree.

_____ 7. The <u>vacant</u> house rang with the laughter of many visitors.

✔ _____ 8. The paintings were <u>exhibited</u> for the public to view at the museum.

Cumulative Vocabulary Review
Objective: Use vocabulary words *(Comprehension and Vocabulary Skills)*
Extension: Have students rewrite the four unchecked sentences in Part B so that the words are used correctly.
53

Name   Date

A. Choose the synonym for the underlined word in each sentence. Circle the letter of the synonym.

1. Caddie liked to see the sun glisten on the water.
   a. darken   **b.** shine   **c.** fall   **d.** rise

2. Caddie and Warren could only follow along in awkward imitation of Tom's skill.
   a. graceful   **b.** equal   **c.** strange   **d.** clumsy

3. Tom saw that only instant action on his part could save Caddie.
   a. early   **b.** late   **c.** immediate   **d.** proper

4. Mother's expression showed fond concern.
   a. angry   **b.** loving   **c.** irritated   **d.** silly

5. She had been reserving the clocks as a final treat.
   a. working   **b.** reading   **c.** learning   **d.** saving

---

B. Now choose the antonym for the underlined word in each sentence. Circle the letter of the antonym.

1. After the fierce snowstorm, Father took his children to the millpond.
   a. mild   **b.** terrible   **c.** ordinary   **d.** final

2. Warren shrieked his alarm, but there was no time to fetch Father from the mill.
   a. yelled   **b.** whispered   **c.** hollered   **d.** yawned

3. With cool presence of mind, Tom made Warren lie down on the ice.
   a. need   **b.** location   **c.** absence   **d.** collection

4. As Caddie worked on the clock, time slipped away unheeded.
   a. noticed   **b.** luckily   **c.** quickly   **d.** pretty

5. The family was surprised that Caddie had mended Mr. Tanner's clock.
   a. fixed   **b.** held   **c.** used   **d.** broken

"Caddie Woodlawn," *Landscapes* (Hardcover: pages 200-210) *Frontiers* (Softcover: pages 67-74)

Objective: Identify synonyms and antonyms *(Comprehension and Vocabulary Skills)*

Extension: Have students write an antonym and a sentence for *prohibit, minimum, imaginary, combines, accidental,* and *comedy.*

Name _____   Date _____

A. Match each word in Column 1 with its definition in Column 2. Write the letter of the definition on the line before the word.

Column 1	**Column 2**
__c__ 1. opportunities	**a.** showed by example
__e__ 2. concentration	**b.** irritation and anger
__f__ 3. despair	**c.** chances
__b__ 4. exasperation	**d.** very interested
__d__ 5. absorbed	**e.** close attention
__a__ 6. demonstrated	**f.** complete loss of hope

B. Circle the letter of the word that best completes each sentence.

1. Caddie became _____ in watching her brother Tom skate.
   a. demonstrated   (**b.**) absorbed   **c.** opportunities

2. Tom's face showed great _____ as he gracefully cut fancy figures on the ice.
   a. despair   **b.** exasperation   (**c.**) concentration

3. After falling down repeatedly, Caddie became filled with _____.
   a. opportunities   **b.** concentration   (**c.**) despair

4. Then Tom _____ to Caddie how to push and glide across the ice.
   (**a.**) demonstrated   **b.** absorbed   **c.** concentration

5. When she discovered that she too could skate, Caddie was no longer filled with such _____.
   a. concentration   **b.** opportunities   (**c.**) exasperation

6. She hoped that there would be many more _____ for skating before the winter was over.
   (**a.**) opportunities   **b.** despair   **c.** absorbed

"Caddie Woodlawn," *Landscapes* (Hardcover: pages 200-210) *Frontiers* (Softcover: pages 67-74)

Objective: Use vocabulary words *(Comprehension and Vocabulary Skills)*   **Extension:** Have students write a sentence for each word in Part A.

55

Name

Date

A. The events described below are about "Caddie Woodlawn." The events are not in the right order. Number the events in the order in which they happened.

___5___ Caddie developed a bad cold, which kept her in bed for a week.

___8___ Mr. Woodlawn explained and demonstrated while Caddie fixed the clock.

___9___ Caddie never forgot the lesson she learned that day in the attic.

___2___ Caddie fell through the ice and came close to drowning.

___1___ Caddie and her brothers skated on the millpond.

___7___ While she was working on Mr. Tanner's clock, the clock flew into pieces.

___3___ Father wrapped Caddie in buffalo robes and took her home.

___4___ Mother put Caddie into a steaming washtub before the kitchen fire.

___6___ Her wandering feet took Caddie up to the attic where there were several clocks in need of repair.

B. Write complete sentences to answer the following questions about "Caddie Woodlawn." (Answers will vary.)

1. How was Tom able to save Caddie from drowning?

He made Warren lie down on the ice. Catching hold of Warren's feet, Tom pushed Warren

out over the thin ice until he could reach Caddie. Then Tom pulled both Warren and Caddie

to safety.

2. What effect did Caddie's accident have on the way she spent her winter?

Caddie spent the winter at home, recovering from the illness that her accident caused.

To relieve her boredom, she tried to repair Mr. Tanner's clock. This led her to become a partner

in her father's clock-repair business.

3. What do you think was the lesson that Caddie learned that day in the attic?

Caddie learned that she had the ability to fix clocks just like her father did. She also learned

that her father had enough confidence in her to make her his partner when repairing clocks.

MACMILLAN PUBLISHING COMPANY

Name _____ Date _____

Use the prefixes in the box below to complete the crossword puzzle.

| anti- | post- | pro- | dis- | pre- | re- |

ACROSS

1. acting against noise
2. acting against gravity
3. after an election
4. to route again
5. to create again
6. to fail to agree
7. in favor of war

DOWN

3. in favor of America
8. to call back or again
9. after a glacier
10. to measure again
11. lack of order
12. before a season
13. in preparation for a launch

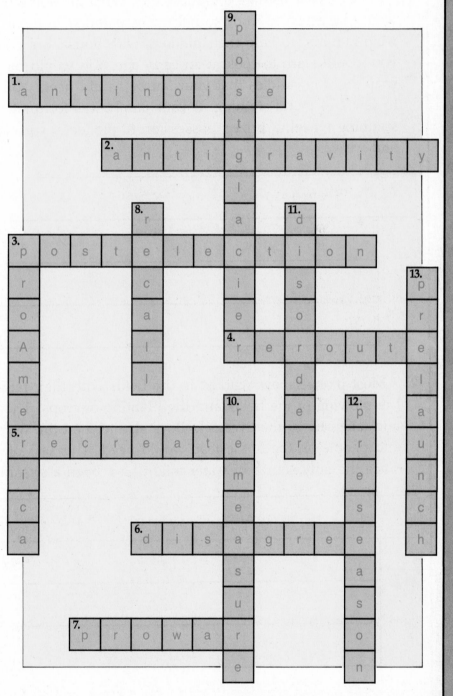

"Caddie Woodlawn," *Landscapes* (Hardcover: pages 200-210) *Frontiers* (Softcover: pages 64-74)

Objective: Identify prefixes: *anti-, pro-, pre-, post-, re-, dis-* (Decoding and Phonics Skills)

Extension: Have students write a paragraph using as many words in the crossword puzzle as they can.

57

Name   Date

A. Read each paragraph. In the first box below the paragraph, write the sentence that states the main idea. Then write three details that support the main idea.
(Students may choose any three supporting details from the paragraph.)

1. Imagine that you are a pioneer girl. What are some of the tasks that you would be expected to do to help your parents? In most pioneer families, girls were required to help their mothers with household chores. As a pioneer girl, you would learn to cook at an early age. You would be expected to make the soap and the candles that your family would need. You would also be taught to sew and mend clothing. If your family was fortunate enough to have a spinning wheel, a prized possession to pioneers, you would also learn to spin and weave.

In most pioneer families, girls helped their mothers with household chores.
Pioneer girls did sewing and mending.
Pioneer girls made soap and candles.
Pioneer girls learned to spin and weave.

2. Most pioneer boys worked in the fields with their fathers. Boys helped with the plowing of the fields and the planting of crops. They helped build fences and take care of the livestock. Boys also fetched the water that both animals and people on the homestead would need. This was often a difficult task since the only source of water might have been a stream several miles away.

Most pioneer boys worked in the fields with their fathers.
Pioneer boys helped with plowing and planting.
Pioneer boys built fences and cared for livestock.
Pioneer boys fetched the water for animals and people.

v

"Frontier Schools," *Landscapes* (Hardcover: pages 216-225) *Frontiers* (Softcover: pages 80-89)

Objective: Distinguish between main idea and supporting details: beginning, middle, or ending sentence *(Comprehension and Vocabulary Skills)*

Extension: Have students rewrite one of the paragraphs on this page so that the main idea is in the last sentence.

58

Name _____   Date _____

A. Read the sentences. Then use the words in the box to complete the sentences below.

geography	memorizing	rigors	scarce	recitation

When our class decided to put on a skit showing what a frontier school was like, we recruited several students from every grade level to participate. During rehearsals, we sat on benches _____ memorizing _____ our parts until it was our turn to speak or act. Ms. Jennings scheduled one night so that our parents could see the skit. When the first graders stood up and gave a

_____ recitation _____ of the alphabet, an applause broke out in one corner and spread through the audience like wildfire. The fourth graders sang a

_____ geography _____ lesson, and our fifth grade class gave a narration

about how _____ scarce _____ supplies such as books, paper, maps, and globes were in a frontier school. The sixth graders wrote and recited a poem

about the daily _____ rigors _____ in the life of a pioneer child. When our skit was over, we received a standing ovation.

B. Write complete sentences to answer the following questions. (Answers will vary.)

1. If you were asked to give a recitation in class, how would you prepare for it?

Answers should suggest that memorization is an important part of preparing for recitation.

2. Suppose you were asked to describe the geography of the area in which you live. What would you say?

Answers should include mention of the climate, the terrain, the resources, and the use of

the land.

3. What are some things that are considered scarce in the area where you live?

_____

_____

_____

"Frontier Schools," *Landscapes* (Hardcover: pages 216-225) *Frontiers* (Softcover: pages 80-89)

Objective: Use vocabulay words *(Comprehension and Vocabulary Skills)*

Extension: Have students prepare a recitation, perhaps by memorizing a poem or a fable. Then have students share their pieces in a recitation period.

Name _____   Date _____

A. Below are some statements about "Frontier Schools." Write **T** if the statement is true. Write **F** if it is false.

___F___ **1.** When the first pioneer families settled in a new area, there were many schools.

___F___ **2.** The children of pioneer families were never taught at home.

___T___ **3.** The first teachers were usually pioneer women with their own families and homes to care for.

___F___ **4.** Each child in a pioneer school had his or her own desk.

___T___ **5.** Frontier schools had no electricity, no plumbing, and no running water.

___T___ **6.** Pioneer children started their day long before school began.

___T___ **7.** Classroom time was spent mostly on reading, writing, and arithmetic.

___F___ **8.** Textbooks were readily available in pioneer schools.

___F___ **9.** A part of each school day was given to science projects.

B. Use complete sentences to answer the following questions about "Frontier Schools." (Answers will vary.)

1. How might a pioneer schoolhouse in one area differ from a schoolhouse in another area?

The schoolhouses sometimes differed in the materials used to build them. Where it was

available, wood was used. But on the prairie, schoolhouses were made from sod.

2. How were all pioneer schoolhouses alike?

They all had dirt floors, unplastered walls, and few windows. There was no electricity,

plumbing, or running water.

3. What did the class do when the teacher said, "Fourth grade, turn, rise, and pass"?

Everybody in that grade would go up to the recitation bench in front and sit there and recite

their lesson.

Name _____ Date _____

A. Decide what each numbered word means. Fill in the circle before your answer.

1. insensitive
   - (a) opposed to being sensitive
   - (b) instead of being sensitive
   - (c) after being sensitive
   - (d) not sensitive

2. preshrunk
   - (a) shrunk later
   - (b) shrunk beforehand
   - (c) instead of being shrunk
   - (d) not shrinkable

3. illiterate
   - (a) not literate
   - (b) against being literate
   - (c) after becoming literate
   - (d) in favor of being literate

4. pro-American
   - (a) before America came to be
   - (b) against America
   - (c) in favor of America
   - (d) not American

5. antifreeze
   - (a) in favor of freezing
   - (b) not frozen
   - (c) after freezing
   - (d) acting against freezing

6. postoperative
   - (a) after an operation
   - (b) before an operation
   - (c) during an operation
   - (d) instead of an operation

7. impassable
   - (a) not able to be passed or traveled
   - (b) able to be passed or traveled
   - (c) not passing or traveling
   - (d) in favor of passing or traveling

8. irresponsible
   - (a) somewhat responsible
   - (b) not responsible
   - (c) in favor of responsibility
   - (d) against responsibility

B. Choose two of the numbered words from Part A and use them in sentences of your own. (Sentences will vary.)

1. _____

   _____

2. _____

   _____

"Frontier Schools," *Landscapes* (Hardcover: pages 216-225) *Frontiers* (Softcover: pages 80-89)

Objective: Identify prefixes: *anti-, pro-, pre-, post-, il-, im-, in-, ir-* *(Decoding and Phonics Skills)*

Extension: Have students use the dictionary to write two words using each prefix in Part A.

61

Name _____   Date _____

A. Read each paragraph. Then circle the letter of the sentence that states the main idea of each paragraph below.

1.   Schools today teach students the basic subjects of reading, writing, and arithmetic. Students today, however, also learn about the world they live in through history, social studies, and science. Schools also help students to enjoy art and music. Today's schools teach more than the basic skills of reading, writing, and arithmetic.

    a. Schools today teach students the basic subjects of reading, writing, and arithmetic.

    b. Students today learn about the world they live in.

    (c.) Today's schools teach more than the basic skills of reading, writing, and arithmetic.

2.   The schools of today are very different from the schools of the frontier. Modern schools are larger than the one room schoolhouses of the 1800s. Today, children sit at desks or tables, but in the pioneer days, the children had to sit on hard benches with no backs to them. There were no water fountains in those times, either. Everyone drank from the bucket in the corner of the schoolroom.

    a. Modern schools are larger than the schoolhouses of the 1800s.

    b. Today's children sit at desks or tables.

    (c.) The schools of today are very different from the schools of the frontier.

3.   Before going to school, pioneer children had many chores to do. Animals had to be fed and given water. The cows also had to be milked and the eggs collected from the chickens. In addition, there might have been wood to chop, land to be worked, and household duties to be done. Life on the frontier was very difficult for the pioneer child. Many of these chores had to be done every day in addition to going to school.

    a. Before going to school, pioneer children had many chores to do.

    (b.) Life on the frontier was very difficult for the pioneer child.

    c. Many of these chores had to be done every day in addition to going to school.

MACMILLAN PUBLISHING COMPANY

"Frontier Schools," *Landscapes* (Hardcover: pages 216-225) *Frontiers* (Softcover: pages 80-89)

Objective: Distinguish between main idea and supporting details: beginning, middle, or ending sentence *(Comprehension and Vocabulary Skills)*

Extension: Have students underline the supporting details for the main idea in each paragraph on this page.

Name   Date

Read each paragraph below. Then underline the generalization that can be drawn from the information presented in the paragraph.

1.   A list of all the portraits of George Washington would fill three volumes. Washington's image has been engraved and used for postage stamps, coins, and dollar bills. His head is one of those carved into Mount Rushmore. Statues of Washington are on display in public squares and government buildings throughout the United States.

   a. More portraits of Washington have been painted than of any other United States President.

   b. George Washington has been a favorite subject of artists.

   c. Washington's portrait appears in many historical volumes.

2. Washington, D.C., is our national capital—the place where elected officials carry on the daily work of running the government. Our national leaders of today work in the White House, the Capitol, and the Supreme Court. But Washington is also a place where people are reminded of the great government leaders of the past. The Washington Monument, the Jefferson Memorial, and the Lincoln Memorial honor three former Presidents whose gifts to the nation will never be forgotten.

   a. Visitors to Washington, D.C., can visit places that will remind them of the great government leaders of the past.

   b. Government officials of today may someday be honored in a special way in Washington, D.C.

   c. Washington, D.C., is a place where today's government officials work and where government leaders of the past are honored.

"Women of the West," *Landscapes* (Hardcover: pages 228-235) *Frontiers* (Softcover: pages 92-99)

Objective: Distinguish between main idea and supporting details: beginning, middle, or ending sentence *(Comprehension and Vocabulary Skills)*

Extension: Have students underline the supporting details for the main idea in each paragraph on this page.

Name   Date

A. Read the clues below. Then use words in the box to complete the crossword puzzle.

agent	management	relatives	depot	generosity

ACROSS

4. act of directing or guiding affairs

5. a railroad station

DOWN

1. willingness to give or share freely

2. person having power to do business for others

3. persons, such as cousins or aunts, connected by family ties

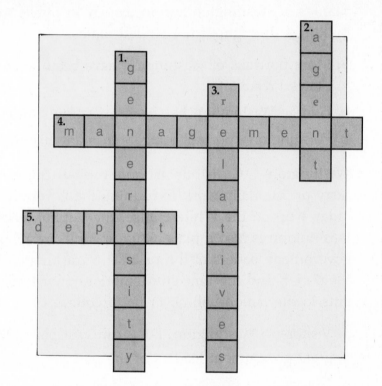

B. Circle the letter of the word that best completes each sentence.

1. If there is no _____ on duty, purchase your tickets aboard the train.
  a. agent   **b.** depot   **c.** generosity

2. In order to keep warm, the passengers waited inside the _____ for the delayed train.
  a. management   **b.** depot   **c.** agent

3. Great-grandmother showed her _____ by giving each of us an antique from her home.
  a. management   **b.** relatives   **c.** generosity

4. Because of poor _____, the railroad was forced to go out of business.
  a. relatives   **b.** management   **c.** depot

Name _____   Date _____

A. Use complete sentences to answer each of the following questions about Clara Brown. (Answers will vary.)

1. Why did Clara Brown leave Kentucky after she had been freed from slavery?

   If she had stayed in a southern state, she might well have been made a slave again.

2. What did Clara Brown do when she heard that a large wagon train was leaving for Colorado?

   She went to see one of the men who was organizing it, and offered to cook and wash in

   exchange for her passage.

3. Give two reasons people were glad to pay Clara for her work.

   (1) She provided a badly needed service.

   (2) She helped people in many ways for which she charged nothing.

4. How was Clara able to make a lot of money?

   She worked long hours, saved carefully, and invested in property.

B. The statements below describe events in the life of Cassie Hill. Number the sentences 1 through 8 to show the order in which the events occurred.

____2____ Cassie's family moved to a ranch in California.

____3____ Cassie married George Hill.

____7____ Cassie took over the job as the Roseville station agent.

____4____ George Hill became station agent and telegraph operator for the town of Hanford.

____6____ Cassie and George moved into the big new depot in Roseville.

____5____ Cassie learned to read Morse code and to operate the telegraph.

____1____ Cassie traveled westward from Iowa in a covered wagon.

____8____ Cassie wrote a poem about her unusual "railroad life."

"Women of the West," *Landscapes* (Hardcover: pages 228-235) *Frontiers* (Softcover: pages 92-99)

Objective: Demonstrate story comprehension *(Comprehension and Vocabulary Skills)*

Name _____ Date _____

Read the paragraph. Then use complete sentences to answer the following questions.

The government of the United States wanted to encourage people to settle the West. It was thought that people would be more eager to move westward if there were railroads. So, in 1850, the government passed several land-grant acts. These acts gave railroads large areas of land on which to build tracks. The railroad companies were quick to take advantage. They built many miles of railroads. Then to offset the building costs, they sold the unused land along the tracks to settlers. With cheap overland transportation available, the land was quickly settled. Towns sprang up along the railroad. There was a sudden burst of trade and industry.

1. What caused the U.S. government to pass the land-grant acts of 1850?

   The government wanted to encourage people to settle the West.

   _____

2. Why did the railroad companies sell the unused land along the tracks to settlers?

   This was done to offset the cost of building the railroads.

   _____

3. What was the effect of the cheap overland transportation that the railroads provided?

   The land was quickly settled; there was a sudden burst of trade and industry.

   _____

"Women of the West," *Landscapes* (Hardcover: pages 228-235) *Frontiers* (Softcover: pages 92-99)

Objective: Identify cause-and-effect relationships: stated or implied (*Comprehension and Vocabulary Skills*)

Extension: Have students write the paragraph on this page using the cause-and-effect signal words: *because, as a result,* and *so.*

Name _____ Date _____

Read each question. Write **encyclopedia, almanac,** or **atlas** to show where you would find the answer most quickly.

1. What is the current population of Colorado?

   almanac _____

2. What is the approximate distance from St. Louis to Fort Loranie?

   atlas _____

3. What role did Captain Robert Gray play in the exploration of the Oregon Territory?

   encyclopedia _____

4. What countries make up Central America?

   atlas _____

5. How is gold formed?

   encyclopedia _____

6. Who is now governor of California?

   almanac _____

7. How much rain fell last year in the state of Washington?

   almanac _____

8. How did Pikes Peak receive its name?

   encyclopedia _____

9. Was last year a leap year?

   almanac _____

10. What is the highest peak in the Rocky Mountains?

    encyclopedia _____

11. What states border Nevada?

    atlas _____

12. How was the first transcontinental railroad built?

    encyclopedia _____

13. What is the address of the Chamber of Commerce in Denver, Colorado?

    almanac _____

14. Where is Switzerland in relation to France?

    atlas _____

15. How many visitors arrived in California last year?

    almanac _____

16. Who is Sally Kristen Ride?

    encyclopedia _____

17. What river divides Paris, France, into two sections?

    atlas _____

18. Who was Edgar Allan Poe?

    encyclopedia _____

"Women of the West," *Landscapes* **(Hardcover: pages 228-235)** *Frontiers* **(Softcover: pages 92-99)**

Objective: Use reference sources: encyclopedia, almanac, atlas *(Study Skills)*

Extension: Have students choose, look up, and write the answer to five questions on this page.

Name _____   Date _____

Read each paragraph. Then circle the letter next to the phrase that best completes the sentence or answers the question.

The Chinooks were one of the many Indian tribes who lived in the Oregon Territory. This group of Indians lived along the lower Columbia River where they fished for salmon. Once explorers arrived in the region, the Chinooks learned quickly how to deal with the newcomers. They taught both the explorers and the early settlers a simplified form of their language and engaged the newcomers in trade. Being skilled carvers, the Chinook Indians were eager for the iron tools that could be gained in exchange for fish or furs.

1. The author probably wrote this passage _____.

    a. to entertain the reader with an Indian myth

    b. to persuade the reader to learn the Chinook language

    c. to explain how the Chinooks adjusted to the settlement of their territory

2. How does the author seem to feel about the Chinooks?

    a. amused by the cleverness of the Chinooks

    b. angry that settlers disturbed the Chinook way of life

    c. impressed by the way the Chinooks adapted

Wagon trains are now forming for anyone interested in having the adventure of a lifetime. You too can start a new life beyond the divide. Come to the rich bottomlands of the Willamette Valley. Leave America for exotic Oregon where crops grow like Jack's beanstalk and where there are so many fish in the rivers that fisherfolk work in twenty-four hour shifts. Only $50 gets you the services of Colonel C. Gorden, as expert a guide to this region as you're likely to find. (Guide must be notified of next of kin in case of emergency.)

3. The author probably wrote this passage _____.

    a. to describe the Oregon Territory for future travelers

    b. to persuade travelers to sign up for a wagon train

    c. to entertain travelers with a funny story

4. How does the author seem to feel about the West?

    a. interested in taking advantage of an opportunity

    b. amused that anyone would want to go there

    c. irritated that he isn't on a wagon train himself

"Saved by a Whisker," *Landscapes* **(Hardcover: pages 238-250)** *Frontiers* **(Softcover: pages 102-114)**

Objective: Identify author's purpose and point of view
(Comprehension and Vocabulary Skills)

Extension: Have students write a paragraph about a wagon train journey with Colonel C. Gordon with the purpose to entertain the reader.

Name _____ Date _____

A. Match each word in the box with its definition by writing the word on the lines below. The word in the puzzle box gives one source of gold.

genuine	detect	financial	courteous	residue

1. substance remaining at the end
2. to discover
3. polite
4. relating to money
5. real; what it appears to be

1. _r_ _e_ _s_ _i_ _d_ _u_ _e_

2. _d_ _e_ _t_ _e_ _c_ _t_

3. _c_ _o_ _u_ _r_ _t_ _e_ _o_ _u_ _s_

4. _f_ _i_ _n_ _a_ _n_ _c_ _i_ _a_ _l_

5. _g_ _e_ _n_ _u_ _i_ _n_ _e_

B. Choose a word from the box above to complete the sentences.

1. It takes experience to know whether gold dust is _____genuine_____ or fake.

2. Many people who went West had their dream of _____financial_____ success destroyed.

3. Special machines were invented to _____detect_____ gold.

4. The _____residue_____ left at the bottom of the miner's pan was not always valuable.

5. In the gold fields, as elsewhere, one could expect good treatment if one was _____courteous_____ and showed good manners.

"Saved by a Whisker," *Landscapes* (Hardcover: pages 238-250) *Frontiers* (Softcover: pages 102-114)

Objective: Use vocabulary words *(Comprehension and Vocabulary Skills)*

Extension: Have students write a paragraph using the words in the box in Part A.

69

Name   Date

A. Below are some statements about "Saved by a Whisker." Write **T** if the sentence is true. Write **F** if it is false.

___T___ **1.** Quartz Jackson wanted to look good when he met his fiancée.

___F___ **2.** Jack wanted to remain in San Francisco.

___F___ **3.** Jack needed to find gold to save the family business.

___F___ **4.** Water in San Francisco cost ten dollars a bucket.

___T___ **5.** A riverboat left every afternoon for Sacramento.

___F___ **6.** The fare to Sacramento City was fifty dollars.

B. Here are the important events that occurred in "Saved by a Whisker." Number the events 1 through 6 to show the order in which they happened. Then using the events write a paragraph summarizing the story on the lines below. (Summaries will vary.)

___6___ Jack and Praiseworthy put up a sign saying, "FREE HAIRCUTS: Miners Only."

___2___ They discovered that the trip to Sacramento would cost twenty-five dollars each.

___4___ Quartz asked Jack who his barber was.

___1___ Jack and Praiseworthy arrived in San Francisco.

___3___ They accused Quartz Jackson, the miner, of following them.

___5___ Quartz paid for his haircut with gold dust.

_____

_____

_____

_____

_____

_____

"Saved by a Whisker," *Landscapes* (Hardcover: pages 238-250) *Frontiers* (Softcover: pages 102-114)

Objective: Demonstrate story comprehension *(Comprehension and Vocabulary Skills)*

Name _____   Date _____

Read the first sentence in each pair. Then fill in the circle next to the letter that completes the second sentence.

1. A telegraph had signaled the arrival of the ship.
   An antonym for arrival is _____.
   (a) coming   (b) voyage   ●c departure   (d) farewell

2. Many people waited on the wharf to meet passengers.
   A synonym for wharf is _____.
   (a) shore   ●b dock   (c) sand   (d) bridge

3. In pioneer days, it was a necessity to get up very early every morning.
   A synonym for necessity is _____.
   (a) possibility   (b) place   (c) time   ●d need

4. Jack and Praiseworthy had very modest needs.
   An antonym for modest is _____.
   ●a expensive   (b) weird   (c) particular   (d) modern

5. Quartz Jackson was mighty peculiar.
   An antonym for peculiar is _____.
   (a) strange   (b) humorous   ●c normal   (d) sad

6. The blossom added cheer to the otherwise dingy hotel room.
   A synonym for blossom is _____.
   (a) color   ●b flower   (c) mirror   (d) smile

7. The journey across the Rockies was a perilous one.
   A synonym for perilous is _____.
   ●a dangerous   (b) pleasant   (c) easy   (d) impossible

8. The miner used an old blanket to form a makeshift tent.
   An antonym for makeshift is _____.
   (a) temporary   ●b permanent   (c) uncomfortable   (d) waterproof

9. At the end of their journey, many pioneers were overcome with weariness.
   A synonym for weariness is _____.
   ●a tiredness   (b) worry   (c) grief   (d) panic

"Saved by a Whisker," *Landscapes* (Hardcover: pages 238-250) *Frontiers* (Softcover: pages 102-114)

Objective: Identify synonyms and antonyms *(Comprehension and Vocabulary Skills)*

Extension: Have students write one synonym and one antonym for the following words. Then have them use the words in a sentence. *(strengthen, positive, defeat, gather)*

Name   Date

A. Read each definition. Then fill in the circle of the word it defines.

1. very interested
  (a) attitude   (b) boarders   (c) absorbed

2. severity; harshness
  (a) rigors   (b) persuasion   (c) recitation

3. relating to money matters
  (a) principal   (b) financial   (c) scarce

4. learning by heart
  (a) sculpture   (b) shelter   (c) memorizing

5. showing good manners
  (a) courteous   (b) expedition   (c) excelled

6. close attention
  (a) demonstrated   (b) concentration   (c) exhibited

B. Read the sentences. Then fill in the circle next to the word that best completes each sentence below.

1. When it comes to adventure, you may have more _____ than you ever dreamed possible.
  (a) opportunities   (b) genuine   (c) generosity   (d) geography

2. Why pound your desk in _____ because you can't afford to go to distant places?
  (a) management   (b) residue   (c) exasperation (d) agent

3. It does not take the _____ of a friend to get you on the road to new experiences.
  (a) relatives   (b) generosity   (c) courteous   (d) financial

4. Nor do you need to depend upon _____ to support your desire.
  (a) agent   (b) management   (c) geography   (d) relatives

5. _____ adventures, and often the best ones, can be found in books.
  (a) financial   (b) absorbed   (c) genuine   (d) scarce

6. Your imagination need not recognize the boundaries of _____.
  (a) despair   (b) geography   (c) rigors   (d) concentration

7. You can be your own travel _____.
  (a) agent   (b) depot   (c) persuasion   (d) recitation

8. Let the _____ of your adventures be your own affair; read a good book!
  (a) financial   (b) concentration   (c) despair   (d) management

Extension: Have students choose ten words on this page that were not chosen as answers to use in sentences of their own.

Name   Date

Read each selection. Then answer the questions by filling in the circle before each answer.

Jack and Rose bought their tickets at the small box office and then followed the line of people into the huge planetarium. They immediately ran toward the front of the theater and found two seats in the second row. Several minutes passed, and then the large room began to darken. Rose gazed up and gasped. Overhead, stars were beginning to appear on the domed ceiling. After the room was completely dark, a woman's voice could be heard. "I want to welcome all of you to the star show here at the Atwood Planetarium," she said. The two young people settled back into their seats, prepared to enjoy the next hour to the fullest.

1. What happened just before Rose looked up?
   (a) The domed ceiling opened.   (b) The room completely darkened.
   (c) The room began to darken.   (d) The ceiling filled with stars.

2. What happened immediately after the room became completely dark?
   (a) Stars appeared overhead.   (b) The audience was welcomed.
   (c) People found their seats.   (d) Rose gasped.

Marnie had never skated in Central Park before, and she was a little nervous. She put her roller skates on and took a few steps. Suddenly, her feet slipped out from under her, and she landed on the ground with a thud. She carefully picked herself up and began down the pathway. She almost ran smack into a woman pushing a baby carriage. A man waved his cane at her as she sped by him. "Watch where you're going! he cried."

Marnie turned to look back at the man. She failed to see the pond ahead of her and landed in the water with a splash. As she slowly got out of the water, a man flashed his camera at her. Marnie asked why he was taking her picture. The man grinned and said, "It'll look great on the front page of tonight's paper."

Marnie couldn't believe it. She was going to be famous—and just because she was a terrible skater!

3. What did Marnie do first after arriving at Central Park?
   (a) She put her skates on.   (b) She fell into a pond.
   (c) She skated into a woman.   (d) She skated down the path.

4. What happened just after Marnie looked back at the old man?
   (a) She had her picture taken.   (b) She skated into a pond.
   (c) The man called out to her.   (d) She became very nervous.

"The Night of the Leonids," *Landscapes* (Hardcover: pages 274-285) *Encounters* (Softcover: pages 10-21)

Objective: Identify sequence of events: explicit or implied *(Comprehension and Vocabulary Skills)*

Extension: Have students make a sequenced list of the events that take place in one of the selections on this page.

Name _____   Date _____

A. Match each word in the box with its definition. Write the word, one letter to a line, after the number of the definition. The boxed word is the name of a heavenly body.

| pollute | abroad | spectacular | inquired | environment |

1. unusually impressive
2. in a foreign land and out of one's country
3. the earth, air, and water of our planet
4. sought information by asking a question or questions
5. to make impure or dirty

1. s p e c t a **c** u l a r
2.   a b r **o** a d
3. e n v i r o n **m** e n t
4.   i n q u i r **e** d
5.   p o l l u **t** e

B. Circle the letter before the word that best completes each sentence.

1. Lewis was returning to New York after having been _____ for a month.
   a. pollute   **b.** inquired   **(c.)** abroad   **d.** environment

2. As his plane flew over New York City, Lewis could see the _____ lights of the skyline.
   a. abroad   **b.** pollute   **(c.)** spectacular   **d.** inquired

3. When Lewis arrived at the airport, he _____ at the information desk about how to get a taxi to Manhattan.
   (a.) inquired   **b.** abroad   **c.** pollute   **d.** spectacular

4. During his ride home, Lewis thought about how he had missed the excitement of the city's _____.
   a. inquired   **b.** pollute   **c.** abroad   **(d.)** environment

5. As he passed Central Park, Lewis noticed signs that encouraged people to use trash receptacles rather than _____ the park.
   a. environment   **b.** abroad   **(c.)** pollute   **d.** inquired

"The Night of the Leonids," *Landscapes* (Hardcover: pages 274-285) *Encounters* (Softcover: pages 10-21)

Objective: Use vocabulary words *(Comprehension and Vocabulary Skills)*

Extension: Challenge students to use the letters in *environment* to make other words. Each word should have at least four letters.

74

Name _____ Date _____

A. Match each sentence beginning with an ending that will make a true statement about "The Night of the Leonids." Write the letter of the ending on the line.

____b____ **1.** Lewis was named after

____e____ **2.** Grandmother wanted Lewis to see

____a____ **3.** Everyone was invited to Central Park by

____c____ **4.** The Leonids were visible from earth once every

____d____ **5.** The Leonids were actually caused by

a. the Commissioner of Parks.

b. his grandfather.

c. thirty-three and one-third years.

d. a comet named Temple-Tuttle.

e. a shower of stars.

B. Below are some questions about "The Night of the Leonids." Write a complete sentence to answer each question. (Answers will vary.)

1. Why was Lewis staying with his grandmother?

His parents had gone abroad and left him in his grandmother's care.

_____

2. What explanation did Lewis's grandmother give for the fact that the Leonids wouldn't pollute the environment?

She said that they would burn up in the atmosphere.

_____

3. Why was Lewis reluctant to fall asleep?

He was afraid that he would not wake up in time to see the Leonids later that evening.

_____

4. Did Lewis and his grandmother get to see the Leonids? How did you know this?

They didn't see the Leonids. An illustration in the story shows that a sudden cloud cover

blocked them from sight.

_____

"The Night of the Leonids," *Landscapes* (Hardcover: pages 274-285) *Encounters* (Softcover: pages 10-21)

Objective: Demonstrate story comprehension *(Comprehension and Vocabulary Skills)*

Name _____ Date _____

Use this part of an index to answer each question below. Fill in the circle before each answer.

Mars, 42-54	Milky Way,
atmosphere of, 42-43	*See* Galaxies
color changes on, 44-45	Moon, 9-15
photographs, 53-54	atmosphere of, 10
Mercury, 69-72	craters, 9
atmosphere of, 69-70	exploration of, 9, 11
photographs, 71-72	of other planets,
Mesosphere,	*See* Satellites, planetary
See Atmosphere of earth	photographs, 14-15
Meteorites, 34-35	relationship to earth, 8
map, 35	Motion, planetary, 2-3

1. On what page or pages should you look to find out about planetary motion?
   (a) 42-54 (b) 9 (c) 71-72 (d) 2-3 ●

2. Under which heading should you look to find information about the Milky Way?
   (a) Galaxies ● (b) Meteorites (c) Satellites (d) Atmosphere of earth

3. On what pages would you find photographs of Mars?
   (a) 71-72 (b) 14-15 (c) 53-54 ● (d) 42-54

4. On what pages should you look to find all the information in the book about the planet Mercury?
   (a) 42-54 (b) 69-70 (c) 69-72 ● (d) 34-35

5. Under which heading should you look to find information about moons of other planets?
   (a) Atmosphere (b) Galaxies (c) Moon (d) Satellites, planetary ●

6. On what page or pages would you find a meteorite map?
   (a) 53-54 (b) 35 ● (c) 34-35 (d) 14-15

"The Night of the Leonids," *Landscapes* (Hardcover: pages 274-285) *Encounters* (Softcover: pages 10-21)

Objective: Identify parts of a book: index, bibliography *(Study Skills)*

Extension: Have students turn to the index in their science textbooks. Then ask them to look up information under one main topic, subtopic, and cross-reference.

Name _____ Date _____

Read the story. Then underline the answer to each question.

"Quick, Noah, take your family into the tunnel," commanded Mr. Beecher. "The authorities are next door, looking for runaway slaves. After you're in the tunnel, find the door with a carved X."

Mr. Beecher didn't need to tell Noah and his family to keep quiet. They were well aware of the risk involved in fleeing to Canada to escape slavery. They had come as far as the Brooklyn home of Henry Ward Beecher, the famed abolitionist. With his help and the help of others like him, the family would find their way to freedom in Canada.

The family found the door with the X and sat down to wait in the dark tunnel. They listened fearfully to a clatter of hooves overhead and muffled voices in the distance. After a while, the door opened. "All's clear," whispered Mr. Beecher.

The family stepped into the dim light of a carriage house. Mr. Beecher handed a parcel to Noah. "Here is some food and a little money. You'll leave tonight from the piers. I've arranged for you to go up the Hudson to Albany with my friend Captain van den Noort. You'll know him by his red beard. Good luck!"

"Thank you. We'll send word when we get to Canada."

1. What is the plot of this story?

  a. Mr. Beecher told Noah and his family to hide in the tunnel as a trick so that the authorities could catch them.

  b. Noah and his family went up the Hudson with Captain van den Noort.

  c. Mr. Beecher hid Noah and his family in the tunnel and helped them in their journey to freedom in Canada.

  d. Noah and his family hid in the tunnel until Mr. Beecher came to get them.

2. What is the mood of this story?

  a. humorous   **b.** joyful   **c.** suspenseful   **d.** depressing

3. When and where does this story take place?

  a. in present-day Brooklyn   **b.** in Albany over 100 years ago

  c. in present-day Canada   **d.** in Brooklyn over 100 years ago

4. From what point of view is this story told?

  a. third person from Noah's point of view

  b. third person by an outside observer

  c. first person from Noah's point of view

  d. third person from Mr. Beecher's point of view

"**The House of Dies Drear**," *Landscapes* (Hardcover: pages 288-300) *Encounters* (Softcover: pages 24-36)

Objective: Identify plot, setting, mood, narrative point of view (*Literature and Language Skills*)

Extension: Have each student write a paragraph describing the incident as if he or she were a member of Noah's family.

Name _____ Date _____

A. Read the clues below. Then use words from the box to complete the crossword puzzle.

extending   enclosed
foundation   mechanism
descended   meander
forlorn

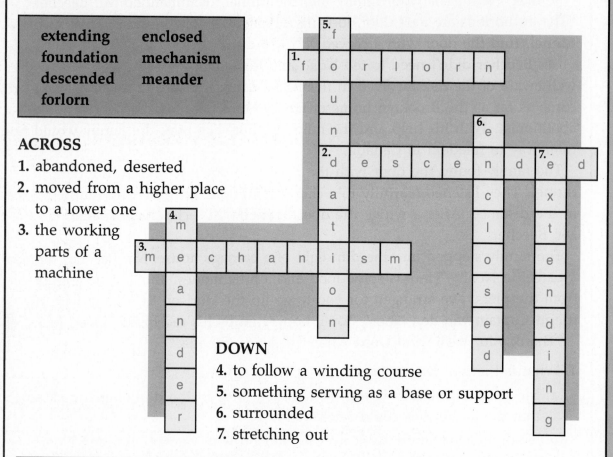

ACROSS

1. abandoned, deserted
2. moved from a higher place to a lower one
3. the working parts of a machine

DOWN

4. to follow a winding course
5. something serving as a base or support
6. surrounded
7. stretching out

B. Use words from the box above to complete these sentences.

1. After the goat chased the chickens, the farmer realized he could not let it

   _____meander_____ about the farm.

2. He decided to build an _____enclosed_____ pen in which the goat could graze.

3. The _____foundation_____ for the pen would, of course, be the ground.

4. _____Extending_____ directly from the barn, the pen would allow the goat to enter the yard whenever he pleased.

5. The first time the farmer put him in his new playground, however, the goat

   had a _____forlorn_____ look on its face.

"**The House of Dies Drear,**" *Landscapes* (Hardcover: pages 288-300) *Encounters* (Softcover: pages 24-36)

Objective: Use vocabulary words (Comprehension and Vocabulary Skills)

Extension: Have students look up the words *descended* and *foundation* in a dictionary to find other meanings. Then have them write a sentence using the meanings they find.

Name

Date

A. Below are some questions about "The House of Dies Drear." Write a complete sentence to answer each one. (Answers will vary.)

1. How did Thomas lose his flashlight in the tunnel?

   He fumbled it, and the flashlight fell to the ground. Then Thomas accidentally kicked it into

   the darkness.

2. What filled Thomas with fear and caused him to run into a wall?

   Thomas was frightened by someone, or something, that made strange wailing noises.

3. Why did Dies Drear make the tunnel under his house meander like a maze?

   Students should suggest that he wanted to confuse any slave catchers who discovered

   the tunnel.

4. If you were Thomas, would you go back to explore the tunnel? Why or why not?

B. The events described below are from "The House of Dies Drear." Number the events from 1-9 to show the order in which they happened.

___6___ Mr. Small explained the tunnel and its history to Thomas.

___3___ Thomas lost his flashlight and tried to find it in the dark.

___8___ Mr. Small told Thomas he had removed the control from the panel.

___1___ Thomas fell into the dark hole under the front steps of the house.

___4___ Something made strange wailing noises in the tunnel.

___7___ Mr. Small investigated the tunnel by himself.

___2___ Thomas went down the rock stairway with his flashlight.

___5___ Thomas screamed for help.

"The House of Dies Drear," *Landscapes* **(Hardcover: pages 288-300)** *Encounters* **(Softcover: pages 24-36)**
Objective: Demonstrate story comprehension *(Comprehension and Vocabulary Skills)*

Name   Date

Read each paragraph and answer the question about it. Circle your answer.

It was Warren's first night alone in the new house. His parents had gone out to a movie, and Warren felt uneasy being all by himself. His nervousness made him hungry, and he looked for something to eat in the kitchen. There was a container of popping corn and a couple of bananas. The idea of popcorn sounded good. Then Warren remembered that the popcorn popper was in the basement and the light in the basement had burned out. He opened the basement door and looked down the stairs. Warren thought he heard a strange noise somewhere in the darkness.

1. What probably happened next?
- **a.** Warren went into the basement and got the popper.
- **b.** Warren didn't eat anything.
- **c.** Warren went straight to bed and fell asleep.
- (**d.**) Warren went back to the kitchen and ate the bananas.

Diane had been running for nearly thirty minutes in the cross country race. The finish line was only a few hundred yards ahead of her. Already several runners had crossed it, but Diane didn't think she had the energy to make the finish. Her legs felt as if there were heavy weights attached to them. Every muscle in her thin body ached. All she wanted to do was collapse on the grass. Then suddenly she saw her whole family near the finish line. They were shouting her name and cheering her on. All at once Diane felt the weights fall from her legs. New energy flowed through her body.

2. What probably happened next?
- **a.** Diane stopped to say hello to her family.
- **b.** Diane collapsed unable to run any farther.
- (**c.**) Diane managed to finish the race.
- **d.** Diane won the race.

"The House of Dies Drear," *Landscapes* (Hardcover: pages 288-300) *Encounters* (Softcover: pages 24-36)

Objective: Predict outcomes *(Comprehension and Vocabulary Skills)*   **Extension:** Have students underline the sentences in each paragraph that helped them to predict each outcome.

Name _____ Date _____

Complete each analogy by filling in the circle next to the word you choose.

1. Sailor is to boat as
   judge is to _____.
   (a) court   (b) law
   (c) lawyer   (d) gavel

2. Telescope is to star as
   microscope is to _____.
   (a) planet   (b) germ
   (c) scientist (d) animal

3. Plant is to stem as
   tree is to _____.
   (a) trunk   (b) leaf
   (c) flower   (d) roots

4. Rich is to wealthy as
   huge is to _____.
   (a) small   (b) tiny
   (c) enormous (d) poor

5. Oil is to well as
   coal is to _____.
   (a) burn   (b) miner
   (c) mine   (d) pick

6. Chimney is to house as
   drawer is to _____.
   (a) fire   (b) handle
   (c) room   (d) desk

7. Branch is to leaf as
   finger is to _____.
   (a) arm   (b) wrist
   (c) palm   (d) fingernail

8. Fin is to rocket as
   rudder is to _____.
   (a) fish   (b) boat
   (c) ocean   (d) swimmer

9. Ancient is to old as
   modern is to _____.
   (a) sleek   (b) antique
   (c) clean   (d) new

10. Polite is to rude as
    help is to _____.
    (a) assist   (b) ignore
    (c) nice   (d) harm

11. Person is to blood as
    tree is to _____.
    (a) leaf   (b) sap
    (c) branch   (d) forest

12. People are to hotel as
    dog is to _____.
    (a) bark   (b) house
    (c) kennel   (d) cage

13. Eyebrows are to eyes as
    mustache is to _____.
    (a) mouth   (b) nose
    (c) face   (d) teeth

14. Giggle is to laugh as
    sob is to _____.
    (a) chuckle (b) cry
    (c) wince   (d) smile

15. Column is to newspaper
    as paragraph is to _____.
    (a) poem   (b) writer
    (c) news   (d) book

16. Pint is to quart
    as quart is to _____.
    (a) gallon   (b) glass
    (c) milk   (d) cream

Skills Activity: Analogies, *Landscapes* **(Hardcover: pages 302-303)** *Encounters* **(Softcover: pages 38-39)**
Objective: Complete analogies *(Comprehension and Vocabulary Skills)*   **Extension:** Have students write three analogies using some of the words on this page.

Name _____   Date _____

Read the story. Then underline the best answer to each question.

Danielle ran lightly over the drawbridge into the courtyard of the castle. Her brother Tim followed, carrying their little sister Chrissy. Chrissy's head was buried in Tim's shoulder.

With shining eyes, Danielle gazed around at the ancient walls. "I've never seen anything so beautiful," she exclaimed.

Danielle took the trembling Chrissy from Tim. "Look how pretty the castle is, Chrissy."

"No," shouted Chrissy as she hid her face in Danielle's neck and began to cry.

Tim patted Chrissy on the back. "It's OK, Chris. Nothing is going to hurt you here."

Tim looked at his feet as he kicked a stone. He said to Danielle, "I've seen enough old buildings during this trip. I want to go home and watch football. All you can see in Europe is soccer."

"You can watch football anytime," Danielle said, "but you can't see this when you're at home."

1. How does Danielle feel in the story?

   a. worried   **b.** grateful   **c.** awed   **d.** amused

2. Why do you think she feels this way?

   a. She's seen the castle many times before.

   b. She likes her brother's and sister's company.

   c. She wants Chrissy to stop crying.

   d. She's never seen a castle like this before.

3. How does Tim feel in the story?

   a. bored   **b.** excited   **c.** upset   **d.** jealous

4. How do you know how Tim feels?

   a. from the way the author describes him

   b. from what Danielle says

   c. from what he says

   d. from his thoughts

5. Chrissy seems frightened of the castle. How can you tell?

   a. Chrissy buries her head in Tim's shoulder.

   b. Chrissy shouts at Danielle.

   c. Tim carries Chrissy into the courtyard.

   d. from what Tim says to Chrissy

"A Game of Catch," *Landscapes* **(Hardcover: pages 304-320)** *Encounters* **(Softcover: pages 40-56)**

Objective: Make inferences about a character's motives or feelings
(Literature and Language Skills)

Extension: Have students write a passage with thoughts, descriptions, and dialogue about one of the following: a picnic, a day at the beach, or an afternoon at the movies.

MACMILLAN PUBLISHING COMPANY

Name   Date

A. Read the clues. Then use words from the box to complete the crossword puzzle.

| circumference | tinged | intent | anonymous | segments | nimbly |

ACROSS
2. line around something
4. slightly colored
5. lightly and quickly
6. divisions; sections

DOWN
1. of unknown origin
3. firmly directed or fixed

Crossword:
2 across: circumference
4 across: tinged
5 across: nimbly
6 across: segments
2 down: cintent (intent)
1 down: anonymous

B. Circle the letter before the word that best completes each sentence.

1. Kate was _____ on arriving at the castle by sundown.
   a. nimbly   b. anonymous   **c. intent**   d. tinged

2. She noticed that the sky was already becoming _____ with red and orange.
   a. segments   b. circumference   **c. tinged**   d. nimbly

3. Kate looked at an old globe and tried to measure the _____ of the earth.
   a. intent   b. anonymous   **c. circumference**   d. tinged

4. The castle had been built by an _____ lord in the twelfth century.
   a. segments   b. circumference   **c. anonymous**   d. nimbly

5. Kate entered a huge courtyard that had been divided into three _____.
   a. tinged   b. nimbly   **c. segments**   d. intent

6. She ran _____ up the stairs to the nearest parapet and watched the sun go down.
   a. nimbly   b. segments   c. anonymous   d. intent

"A Game of Catch," *Landscapes* (Hardcover: pages 304-320) *Encounters* (Softcover: pages 40-56)

Objective: Use vocabulary words (Comprehension and Vocabulary Skills)

Extension: Have students write sentences using the words in the box in Part A.

83

Name _____   Date _____

A. Below are some statements about "A Game of Catch." Write **T** if the statement is true. Write **F** if it is false.

_T_ 1. The children in the painting were dressed for winter.

_T_ 2. Mr. Whittaker believed that the children in the picture traveled through time.

_F_ 3. This story takes place in the eighteenth century.

_F_ 4. Mr. Wittaker thought there was a big difference between seeing and imagining.

_T_ 5. Kate and Hugh were moving to Canada for five years.

_F_ 6. Kate told her brother that she had played catch with the children from the picture.

B. Below are some questions about "A Game of Catch." Write a complete sentence to answer each. (Answers will vary.)

1. Why did Kate want to see the children from the picture so badly?

Kate wanted to see the children because it would prove that Hugh had been wrong about the

children's ability to communicate with her.

2. How did Mr. Wittaker know that the children from the picture had been with Kate on the ice?

When Mr. Wittaker looked at the painting, the children were gone from it.

3. Why did Kate throw the ball back to the children?

Kate threw the ball back because she realized that the children could not return to their own

time without it.

4. How and why had the picture changed by the end of the story?

By the end of the story, the girl, rather than the boy, was holding the ball. Kate had thrown the

ball back to the girl during their game of catch.

Name _____ Date _____

Read each paragraph. Then answer each question below it. (Answers will vary.)

Arthur had been waiting for weeks for the ice on the lake to freeze. There had been two weeks of continuously freezing temperatures. Today, Arthur thought, the ice should be hard enough to skate on.

1. What do you think Arthur will do next?

Arthur will probably dress warmly, get his skates, and go to the lake.

When Arthur arrived at the lake, he walked out on the ice in his boots. He jumped up and down a few times to see if the ice would support his weight. The ice seemed solid enough to him.

2. What do you think Arthur will do next?

Arthur will probably put his skates on and skate on the lake.

Arthur glided smoothly out to the center of the lake. Since he had the entire lake to himself, he tried some fancy skating. In the middle of a turn, he fell hard. He heard the ice crack and groan under the weight of his fall. As he picked himself up, he realized that the ice might not be thick enough to skate on safely.

3. What do you think Arthur will do next?

Arthur will probably get off the ice.

After Arthur had finished taking his skates off, he noticed a group of smaller children playing on the ice on the other side of the lake. He tried to yell a warning to them that the ice wasn't safe. The group of children didn't seem to hear him.

4. What do you think Arthur will do next?

He will probably walk around the lake and tell the children that the ice isn't safe.

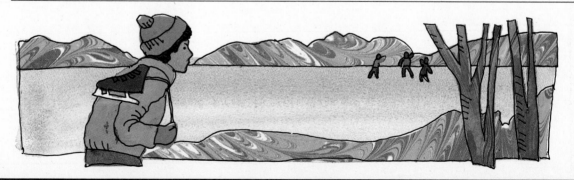

"A Game of Catch," *Landscapes* **(Hardcover: pages 304-320)** *Encounters* **(Softcover: pages 40-56)**

Objective: Predict outcomes *(Comprehension and Vocabulary Skills)*

Extension: Have students change one of their predictions and rewrite the remainder of the story to agree with the change.

Name   Date

Read the selection. Then answer the questions about the characters' motives and feelings. (Answers will vary.)

The small rubber raft moved slowly down the narrow river. It picked up speed as it headed toward the rushing waters of the rapids. Hank looked at the rapids and tightened his trembling fingers around his metal paddle. Beads of sweat formed on his tanned forehead. He had never shot the rapids before.

"Maybe we should turn back," he said hoarsely to the other two people in the raft.

"Don't be silly!" cried Marge. "It's too late to do that. Anyway, this is the best part of the whole trip!"

Ted, who sat behind Marge, smiled. "Relax, Hank," he said in a soft voice. "We'll be over the worst part in a minute or so." Then he covered a yawn with one large hand and tried to concentrate on the business at hand.

1. How did Hank feel about shooting the rapids?

frightened, anxious

2. How do you know?

Hank's fingers were trembling and his forehead was sweaty; he asked if the others wanted

to turn back.

3. Why did Hank feel as he did?

He has never gone down rapids in a raft before.

4. How did Marge feel?

excited

5. What helped you figure out how Marge felt?

Marge said that she didn't want to turn back, and that they were about to experience the best

part of the whole trip.

6. How did Ted feel?

relaxed, complacent

7. What helped you figure out how Ted felt?

He covered a yawn and tried to concentrate on the business at hand.

"Canyon Winter," *Landscapes* **(Hardcover: pages 326-339)** *Encounters* **(Softcover: pages 62-75)**

Objective: Make inferences about a character's motives or feelings
(Literature and Language Skills)

Extension: Have students write paragraphs describing how they would feel if they were with Hank, Marge, and Ted in the rubber raft.

Name _____   Date _____

A. Match each word in the box with its definition. Write the word, one letter to a line, after the number of the definition. The word in the box is the name of a body of water.

privacy	abruptly	plight	deserted	intruded	indication

1. entered without being asked or wanted
2. a bad situation or condition

3. the state of being secluded, isolated
4. left alone or abandoned
5. suddenly or unexpectedly

1. i n t **r** u d e d
2.   p l **i** g h t
3. p r i **v** a c y
4. d e s **e** r t e d
5.   a b **r** u p t l y

B. Circle the letter before the word that best completes each sentence.

1. The shadows that fell across the canyon were a good _____ that night was on its way.
   (a.) indication   **b.** plight   **c.** deserted   **d.** privacy

2. The old man enjoyed his _____ in the canyon, far away from other people.
   a. deserted   **b.** abruptly   **(c.)** privacy   **d.** indication

3. The water rose _____ and overturned the small boat.
   a. intruded   **b.** plight   **c.** deserted   **(d.)** abruptly

4. The cabin had been _____ by the campers and remained empty all winter.
   (a.) deserted   **b.** indication   **c.** abruptly   **d.** intruded

5. The bear cub's _____ was to be stuck in a tree with no way to get down.
   a. privacy   **(b.)** plight   **c.** deserted   **d.** abruptly

6. When we were camping, a raccoon _____ upon us by getting into our food supplies.
   a. plight   **b.** indication   **(c.)** intruded   **d.** privacy

"Canyon Winter," *Landscapes* (Hardcover: pages 326-339) *Encounters* (Softcover: pages 62-75)

Objective: Use vocabulary words *(Comprehension and Vocabulary Skills)*

Extension: Have students write a sentence for each word in the box in Part A.

87

Name _____ Date _____

A. The events described below are about "Canyon Winter." Number the events from 1-10 to show the order in which they occurred. Write the numbers on the lines.

___4___ Peter climbed up on to a huge boulder and considered his plight.

___10___ Peter promised Omar Pickett he wouldn't try to run away again.

___1___ Peter put food in the spare sleeping bag and ran for the river.

___6___ Omar Pickett leaped into the rushing water to get to Peter.

___3___ The current dragged Peter down and tore off his sleeping bag.

___7___ Omar Pickett looped the rope around Peter and tied the other end around himself.

___9___ Omar Pickett and Peter rested in the sun against a rock wall.

___5___ Omar Pickett found Peter hunched up on the boulder.

___2___ Peter waded into the river with his sleeping bag.

___8___ Peter pulled himself to safety with the rope around him.

B. Below are some questions about "Canyon Winter." Write complete sentences to answer them. (Answers will vary.)

1. Why did Peter try to get across the river and out of the canyon despite the bad conditions?

He wanted desperately to get back home to his family.

2. How did Omar Pickett use the rope to get to Peter after it fell into the water?

He tied one end to a rock and the other end around himself. Then he leaped into the water

and let the current carry him to Peter's rock.

3. Do you think Peter will now mind staying in the canyon with Omar Pickett? Why or why not?

Students will probably suggest that each will be more concerned about the other's feelings in

the future.

"Canyon Winter," *Landscapes* (Hardcover: pages 326-339) *Encounters* (Softcover: pages 62-75)
Objective: Demonstrate story comprehension *(Comprehension and Vocabulary Skills)*

Name _____ Date _____

Read each sentence. Write the base word of the underlined word. Then write a definition for the base word. (Wording will vary.)

1. The horse <u>unseated</u> Carol while she was riding in the mountains.

seat—to place on something; to sit on

_____

2. The two girls listened <u>fearfully</u> to the wolves' howling in the distance.

fear—a strong feeling caused by knowing that danger, pain, or evil is near

_____

3. The marshall caught the man who was <u>illegally</u> hunting deer.

legal—permitted by law

_____

4. We were <u>unsuccessful</u> in our attempt to reach the mountaintop.

success—attainment of a desired end

_____

5. The guide <u>misinformed</u> the tourists about the location of the campground.

inform—to give facts about something

_____

6. The electric typewriter <u>predated</u> the word processor.

date—to belong to a particular time or era

_____

7. Tim felt <u>hopelessly</u> lost as he tried to find his way in the woods.

hope—a strong wish and belief that a thing will happen

_____

8. The family had <u>unknowingly</u> camped in a wildlife sanctuary.

know—to be aware of

_____

"Canyon Winter," *Landscapes* (Hardcover: pages 326-339) *Encounters* (Softcover: pages 62-75)

Objective: Identify base words: two or more affixes *(Decoding and Phonics Skills)*

Extension: Have students use each base word above to create another word by adding two different affixes to it.

Name   Date

Choose a word from the box to match each definition. Write the letters of the word on the lines. Then use the numbers under the letters to discover one of the themes of the first four selections in Unit 3.

privacy	inquired	forlorn	meander	anonymous	nimbly
enclosed	pollute	indication	intent	spectacular	

1. abandoned, deserted f o r l o r n
                        3   1

2. of unknown origin a n o n y m o u s
                            8

3. to make impure or dirty p o l l u t e
                                    15

4. the state or condition of being secluded p r i v a c y
                                             16 11

5. to follow a winding course m e a n d e r
                                  4   17

6. a sign i n d i c a t i o n
           5   9

7. surrounded e n c l o s e d
                        6

8. lightly and quickly n i m b l y
                        13

9. firmly directed or fixed i n t e n t
                             2   14

10. asked i n q u i r e d
                        10

11. impressive s p e c t a c u l a r
                  12   7

l i f e   i s   a n
1 2 3 4   5 6   7 8

a d v e n t u r e
9 10 11 12 13 14 15 16 17

Cumulative Vocabulary Review

Objective: Use vocabulary words *(Comprehension and Vocabulary Skills)*

Extension: Have students write synonyms for as many of the words on the page as they can.

90

Name   Date

Read each selection. Then fill in the circle before the best answer for each question.

Old Bill Moffat had lived alone on a desert island for five long years after being shipwrecked. He had managed to build a life for himself on the lonely island. One morning, Bill saw black smoke in the distance. It was a ship! It was coming to rescue him! Bill tore his shirt off and waved it wildly in the air. Then he turned to look at his little grass hut on the beach. It had been a good, if lonely, life. He would miss many things about it. But he knew now he could never go on living there. He began to wave his shirt again, but with less excitement than before.

1. How did Bill feel about being rescued?
   (a) very unhappy about having to return to the real world
   (b) wildly happy about escaping from the island
   (c) happy, but also a little sad about leaving the island
   (d) unable to feel anything but emptiness

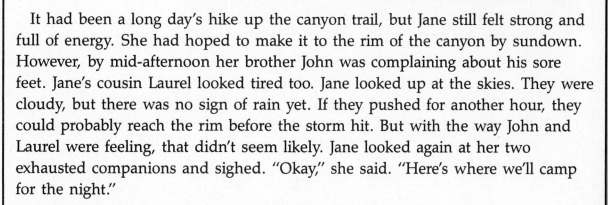

It had been a long day's hike up the canyon trail, but Jane still felt strong and full of energy. She had hoped to make it to the rim of the canyon by sundown. However, by mid-afternoon her brother John was complaining about his sore feet. Jane's cousin Laurel looked tired too. Jane looked up at the skies. They were cloudy, but there was no sign of rain yet. If they pushed for another hour, they could probably reach the rim before the storm hit. But with the way John and Laurel were feeling, that didn't seem likely. Jane looked again at her two exhausted companions and sighed. "Okay," she said. "Here's where we'll camp for the night."

2. What was Jane's motive for stopping early for camp?
   (a) She wanted to give her brother and cousin a rest.
   (b) The weather looked bad for hiking.
   (c) She was tired and couldn't walk another step.
   (d) She had lost her sense of direction.

Skills Activity: Character's Motives or Feelings, *Landscapes* (Hardcover: pages 340-341) *Encounters* (Softcover: pages 76-77)

Objective: Make inferences about a character's motives or feelings *(Literature and Language Skills)*

Extension: Have students rewrite one of the paragraphs to reflect another answer listed on the page.

91

Name _____   Date _____

Read each selection. Then write the answer to each question below.

Astronaut Pat Morgan checked the monitors on the instrument panel as her small rocket landed on the unexplored planet. As she unbuckled her safety belt, Morgan recalled her orders. She was to observe the planet from the inside of her ship before exploring the planet's surface. If the planet appeared to be unsafe, she had orders to blast-off at once and travel to the next planet. The astronaut checked the atmosphere meter. It was green. This meant that the air outside was safe to breathe. Then she slid open a window on the ship and looked out. Outside, there were trees and grass. The place looked very inviting.

1. What do you think Pat Morgan did next?

She probably left the rocket to explore the planet.

2. How do you know?

Pat had observed the planet from the rocket ship and it appeared to be safe. Therefore, she

was probably allowed to explore the planet.

As Mrs. Wallingford handed a check to the repairman, he said, "If you have any more problems with X1000, don't hesitate to call me."

The robot came into the living room carrying breakfast on a tray. "Here's your breakfast, ma'am," said the robot.

"Isn't it time for lunch, X1000?" she asked the robot.

The robot blinked its green eyes. "Of course," it exclaimed. "How silly of me! I'll go get your lunch at once."

"Please don't bother," said the woman. "I'm going shopping and won't be back for hours."

"Let me get your umbrella so you won't get wet," offered the robot helpfully.

Mrs. Wallingford looked out the window and saw that the sun was shining brightly. Then she gazed at the robot. Something was very wrong, she decided.

3. What do you think probably happened next?

Mrs. Wallingford called the repairman to fix her robot.

4. How do you know?

The robot wasn't acting properly, and Mrs. Wallingford decided that there was something

wrong with it.

"C.L.U.T.Z.," *Landscapes* (Hardcover: pages 342-354) *Encounters* (Softcover: pages 78-90)

Objective: Predict outcomes *(Comprehension and Vocabulary Skills)*   **Extension:** Have students write a paragraph explaining what they would do if they owned X1000 and couldn't call a repairperson.

Name _____   Date _____

A. Read the selection below. Write a word from the box to finish each incomplete sentence.

| intercepted | leisure | artificial | primitive | exterior | penetrating |

Our family has had a lot more _____leisure_____ time since Robby came to live with us. Robby is a robot and can do just about anything. Unlike earlier, more _____primitive_____ robots, Robby has been programmed to do the most difficult tasks. He does the housework for my mother and helps my father with his business. He can even help me do my homework. Although he's only _____artificial_____, we think of Robby as just another member of the family.

The other day, as I was walking home with Robby, we were _____intercepted_____ by Fred, the neighborhood bully. Fred began to make jokes about Robby. When I told Fred to stop, he insulted Robby even more.

Robby's metal _____exterior_____ started to vibrate, and his red eyes flashed angrily. He lifted Fred with his two steel arms into the air and stared at him with _____penetrating_____ eyes.

"Why don't you pick on someone your own size?" said Robby. Fred was scared and said he was sorry. Robby put him down and he ran straight home. Robby is handy to have around—in any situation!

_____

B. Use each pair of words in a sentence. (Sentences will vary.)

1. artificial/leisure _____

_____

2. penetrating/primitive _____

_____

3. intercepted/exterior _____

_____

"C.L.U.T.Z.," *Landscapes* (Hardcover: pages 342-354) *Encounters* (Softcover: pages 78-90)

Objective: Use vocabulary words *(Comprehension and Vocabulary Skills)*

Extension: Have each student write a paragraph about having his or her own imaginary robot and the amazing things the robot can do. Ask them to use at least three words from the box in Part A.

93

Name   Date

A. Below are some questions about "C.L.U.T.Z." Use complete sentences to answer each question. (Answers will vary.)

1. What challenge did Taurus Johnson make to Rodney to prove whose robot was better?

He challenged Rodney and Clutz to a game of moonball, robot against robot.

2. What enabled the players of moonball to lift the heavy ball?

They could lift it because the game was played in one-sixth earth's gravity, which made the

ball lighter.

3. Do you think Clutz and Slick were well named? Explain your answer.

Students may suggest that they were well named because Clutz was awkward and clumsy and

Slick was graceful.

4. Describe a contest in which Clutz might beat Slick.

_____

_____

_____

_____

B. Each quotation in Column 1 is from the story "C.L.U.T.Z." Match the quotation with the character in Column 2.

Column 1

___c___ **1.** "Clutz is a great robot. He can do anything any other robot can."

___e___ **2.** "Out of my way, primitive mechanism."

___b___ **3.** "There are no limits to a robot's duty. We serve humanity any and every way we can."

___a___ **4.** "I know a good scrap dealer, if you want to get rid of that thing."

___d___ **5.** "I never saw anybody get stuck on a moonball ring before. I wouldn't have missed it for anything."

Column 2

a. Taurus Johnson
b. Clutz
c. Rodney Pentax
d. Teri Khan
e. Slick

MACMILLAN PUBLISHING COMPANY

"C.L.U.T.Z.," *Landscapes* (Hardcover: pages 342-354) *Encounters* (Softcover: pages 78-90)
Objective: Demonstrate story comprehension (Comprehension and Vocabulary Skills)
94

Name   Date

Circle the letter before the word that best completes each analogy.

1. Sweet is to sour as strong is to _____.
   a. powerful   b. salty
   c. weak   d. small

2. Give is to share as hurt is to _____.
   a. injure   b. help
   c. lose   d. take

3. Bone is to skeleton as minute is to _____.
   a. hour   b. clock
   c. second   d. body

4. Necklace is to bead as forest is to _____.
   a. park   **b. tree**
   c. country   d. campfire

5. Trail is to path as picture is to _____.
   a. frame   b. road
   c. art   **d. painting**

6. Thanksgiving is to holiday as baseball is to _____.
   a. football   b. player
   c. sport   d. bat

7. Water is to swim as air is to _____.
   a. gas   b. airplane
   c. fall   **d. fly**

8. Clear is to cloudy as grumpy is to _____.
   a. wise   b. good
   c. unhappy   **d. cheerful**

9. Mammal is to bear as reptile is to _____.
   a. bird   **b. snake**
   c. animal   d. living thing

10. Cloud is to sky as island is to _____.
    a. ocean   b. city
    c. land   d. ship

11. Cat is to fur as porcupine is to _____.
    a. tail   b. whiskers
    c. quills   d. animals

12. Blanket is to wool as window is to _____.
    a. warm   **b. glass**
    c. frame   d. air

13. Lightning is to bright as thunder is to _____.
    a. dark   b. cloudy
    c. rain   **d. loud**

14. Frog is to tadpole as deer is to _____.
    a. fawn   b. brown
    c. green   d. doe

15. Cowboy is to rodeo as clown is to _____.
    a. horse   b. lasso
    c. tricks   **d. circus**

16. Fruit is to bowl as flowers are to _____.
    a. garden   b. tree
    c. vase   d. buds

"C.L.U.T.Z.," *Landscapes* (Hardcover: pages 342-354) *Encounters* (Softcover: pages 78-90)
Objective: Complete analogies *(Comprehension and Vocabulary Skills)*   **Extension:** Have students describe how the words in each analogy are related.

95

Name   Date

Read the story. Then use complete sentences to answer the questions.

Long ago in ancient Greece, there lived a girl named Arachne. Arachne was so skillful at weaving that she boasted that she was a better weaver than the goddess Athena.

When Athena heard Arachne's boast, she disguised herself as an old woman and went to Arachne's house to speak to her.

"I am an old and experienced woman," Athena said. "I've heard about your boast to Athena and think you are foolish to challenge a goddess."

"Be quiet, old woman," Arachne replied. "I wish Athena would come here so that all could see that I am the better weaver."

Suddenly, Athena threw off her disguise. Too late, Arachne realized how insane her challenge was.

Athena and Arachne both began to weave. When they were finished, Arachne saw the superiority of Athena's work.

Athena turned to her and said, "I am going to punish you as a warning to others who may dare to challenge the gods. From now on, you will be an insect that will always weave a beautiful web."

At this, Arachne shrank into a spider, crawled into a corner, and immediately began to spin a web.

1. What is the setting of this story?

The story takes place at Arachne's house in ancient Greece.

2. What are the most important events in the plot?

Arachne boasts that she is a better weaver than Athena. Athena disguises herself and tries to

warn Arachne about challenging a goddess. When Arachne persists in her challenge, she and

Athena have a contest. Athena wins and changes Arachne into a spider.

3. What is the narrative point of view of the story?

The story is told as a third person narrative by an outside observer.

4. What is the story's mood?

The mood is suspenseful; the reader wonders what will happen next.

"The Flight of Icarus," *Landscapes* **(Hardcover: pages 358-364)** *Encounters* **(Softcover: pages 94-100)**
Objective: Identify plot, setting, mood, narrative point of view *(Literature and Language Skills)*

Extension: Have students write myths of their own that explain other insects, animals, or phenomena in nature.

96

MACMILLAN PUBLISHING COMPANY

Name   Date

A. Find the words whose definitions are given in the word puzzle below. The words are listed up and down, diagonally, and backwards. Write the words on the line next to the definition.

poised	**1.** held in balance
securely	**2.** firmly; tightly; in a stable way
caution	**3.** care with regard to danger or risk
moderate	**4.** kept within reasonable limits
misgivings	**5.** feeling of doubt or uneasiness

```
b  m  e  d  l  m  z  p  m  f  h
t  u  s  e  d  r  i  l  a  e  g
v  m  i  s  g  i  v  i  n  g  s
p  o  o  i  e  w  a  z  c  r  t
g  d  p  o  i  c  o  u  b  c  e
s  e  l  p  v  l  u  d  h  j  k
h  r  s  i  r  p  n  r  x  t  n
c  a  u  t  i  o  n  w  e  r  o
b  t  g  j  q  f  d  u  a  l  n
d  e  k  m  p  r  s  y  m  d  y
```

B. Read each sentence. Fill in the circle next to the word that best completes each sentence.

1. The ancient Greeks believed in being _____ in their daily lives; they tried not to eat or drink too much.
ⓐ poised   **ⓑ moderate**   ⓒ securely   ⓓ caution

2. Apollo, the Greek sun God, had _____ about allowing his son Phaethon drive the fiery chariot of the sun.
ⓐ securely   ⓑ moderate   ⓒ poised   **ⓓ misgivings**

3. The Parthenon is an ancient temple _____atop a hill in Athens, Greece.
ⓐ misgivings   ⓑ caution   ⓒ securely   **ⓓ poised**

4. Anyone entering Minos's maze had to do so with great _____ so that the man-eating Minotaur would not devour him.
ⓐ securely   ⓑ misgivings   ⓒ poised   **ⓓ caution**

5. In one Greek myth, Zeus bound Prometheus _____ to a rock as a punishment for giving fire to mankind.
ⓐ caution   ⓑ moderate   **ⓒ securely**   ⓓ misgivings

"The Flight of Icarus," *Landscapes* **(Hardcover: pages 358-364)** *Encounters* **(Softcover: pages 94-100)**

Objective: Use vocabulary words *(Comprehension and Vocabulary Skills)*   **Extension:** Have students write sentences using the five words in Part A.

97

Name _____   Date _____

A. Match each item in the left column with its description on the right. Write the letter of the description on the line.

__e__ **1.** Crete   **a.** king of Crete

__d__ **2.** Icarus   **b.** architect who built a maze

__g__ **3.** Apollo   **c.** island Daedalus and Icarus flew over

__a__ **4.** Minos   **d.** son of Daedalus

__f__ **5.** Sicily   **e.** island where Daedalus was held prisoner

__b__ **6.** Daedalus   **f.** place Daedalus escaped to

__c__ **7.** Samos   **g.** Greek god that Daedalus built a temple to

B. Write a complete sentence to answer each question below about "The Flight of Icarus." (Answers will vary.)

1. Why did Daedalus make the wax wings?

He needed them to escape from the island of Crete, where Minos held him prisoner.

2. How would watching birds in flight help Icarus fly?

Learning how birds soared and glided would show Icarus how to move when he flew.

_____

3. How did the sun cause Icarus's death?

Its heat softened the wax that held the feathers to the wings. When the wax became so soft

that the feathers fell out, Icarus fell to his death.

4. How did Daedalus keep the memory of his son alive?

He named the land where he buried his son, Icaria.

5. How else might Daedalus and Icarus have escaped from Crete?

_____

_____

_____

Name   Date

A. Find the base word in each key word below. Circle your answer.

1. prefinished	fin	(finish)	finished
2. northerner	the	northern	(north)
3. impatiently	(patient)	pat	impatient
4. entertainers	enter	(entertain)	entertainer
5. reproduces	rod	reproduce	(produce)
6. trimonthly	(month)	trim	monthly
7. unthankful	thankful	(thank)	than
8. biyearly	ear	(year)	early
9. mismatched	mismatch	mat	match
10. unreachable	(reach)	each	reachable

B. A final *e* in many base words is sometimes dropped before adding certain suffixes. The base words in the words below are words of this kind. Each word is made up of a base word, a prefix, and a suffix. Draw a line under each prefix and suffix. Then write the base word on the line.

1. removable   move

2. impurity   pure

3. unfortunate   fortune

4. disapproval   approve

5. nonofficial   office

6. insensitive   sense

"The Flight of Icarus," *Landscapes* (Hardcover: pages 358-364) *Encounters* (Softcover: pages 94-100)

Objective: Identify base words: two or more affixes (*Decoding and Phonics Skills*)

Extension: Have students add affixes to the following words: *natural, pleasant, fail, fancy, guard.*

Name   Date

A. Use this bibliography to answer the questions below. Fill in the circle next to each answer.

> Bowra, C.M. Classical Greece. New York: Time, Inc., 1965.
> Hamilton, Edith. Mythology. Boston: Little, Brown, and Co., 1942.
> Stobart, J.C. The Glory That Was Greece. New York: Grove Press, 1962.

1. Which book was written by Edith Hamilton?
   - (a) The Glory that was Greece
   - (b) Mythology
   - (c) Classical Greece
   - (d) Book of the Ancient Greeks

2. In what year was Classical Greece published?
   - (a) 1959
   - (b) 1961
   - (c) 1962
   - (d) 1965

3. Who is the author of The Glory That Was Greece?
   - (a) Edith Hamilton
   - (b) J.C. Stobart
   - (c) Martin P. Nilsson
   - (d) C.M. Bowra

B. Use this index to answer the questions below. Fill in the letter before your answer.

> Pallas Athena, 27   paradise, 99, 131, 133
>   See Minerva   Parnassus, Mt., 16, 28
> Pan, 5, 7, 8, 100   Pegasus, 154, 157
>   picture, 101   picture, 158
> Pandora, 15, 17   Plutarch, 204

1. On what page would you find a picture of Pan?
   - (a) 158
   - (b) 101
   - (c) 27
   - (d) 204

2. Under what heading would you find more information about Pallas Athena?
   - (a) Pan
   - (b) Minerva
   - (c) paradise
   - (d) Pandora

3. On what pages would you find information about Mt. Parnassus?
   - (a) 16, 28
   - (b) 15, 17
   - (c) 154, 157
   - (d) 99, 131, 133

Skills Activity: Parts of a Book, *Landscapes* **(Hardcover: pages 366-367)** *Encounters* **(Softcover: pages 102-103)**
Objective: Use parts of a book: index, bibliography *(Study Skills)*   **Extension:** Have students write bibliographic entries using each of their textbook titles.
100

Name _____   Date _____

Read the story. Then number the events below in the order in which they occurred.

The Douglas family was eating breakfast when they heard about the hurricane on the radio. The announcer said that a hurricane would strike their area around two o'clock that afternoon. He also advised that those who were listening not to leave their homes from noon to four o'clock when the storm would be at its worst.

Mrs. Douglas and Rhonda went immediately to the store to buy tape, canned goods, and extra batteries for the radio and the flashlight. When they returned, Mr. Douglas and Jason put the lawn furniture in the basement. Mrs. Douglas and Rhonda filled the bathtubs with water in case they were without running water because of the storm. Then, the family put masking tape on all the windows in the house. With tape on the windows, the glass wouldn't shatter into tiny pieces if the wind blew the windows in .

It started raining and the wind began to pick up. By one-thirty, the rain was coming down in torrents and the wind was blowing furiously. Already, the wind had blown the branches off many trees. An oak tree in a neighbor's yard had fallen into the street. Around two o'clock, the rain and wind stopped suddenly. Mrs. Douglas explained that the eye, or the center, was now passing over their area. Then the wind and rain began again just as suddenly as it had stopped. After a few more hours, the wind died down and the rain started to taper off. The radio announcer declared that the hurricane was now moving away from their area.

___6___ Around two o'clock, the wind and rain stopped suddenly.

___1___ The Douglas family ate breakfast.

___5___ The family taped all the windows in the house.

___2___ The radio announcer said that the hurricane would strike about two o'clock.

___4___ Mr. Douglas and Jason put the lawn furniture away.

___3___ Mrs. Douglas and Rhonda went to the store.

___7___ The radio announcer said that the hurricane was moving away from the area.

"East of the Sun and West of the Moon," *Landscapes* (Hardcover: pages 368-380) *Encounters* (Softcover: pages 104-116)

Objective: Identify sequence of events: explicit or implied
(Comprehension and Vocabulary Skills)

Extension: Have students rewrite the story on this page using signal words such as *first, next, then,* and *last.*

101

Name _____ Date _____

A. Match each word in the box with its definition. Write the word one letter to a line. The word in the box is a character found in some folk tales.

| propose | delectable | comely | lofty | misfortune |

1. bad luck; ill fortune
2. to put forward for consideration; suggest
3. extending high in the air; towering
4. delicious; highly pleasing or delightful, especially to the taste
5. pleasing in appearance; good-looking

1. m i s f o r t u n e

2. p r o p o s e

3. l o f t y

4. d e l e c t a b l e

5. c o m e l y

B. Read the following sentences. Put a check next to each sentence in which the underlined word is used correctly.

_____ 1. The <u>comely</u> princess couldn't bear to look at herself in the mirror.

__✔___ 2. After a month of camp food, Karen couldn't wait for one of her mother's <u>delectable</u> meals.

_____ 3. Tim wrote a <u>propose</u> to suggest that the class have a fair.

__✔___ 4. Beth decided to <u>propose</u> that the camera club go on a nature hike.

__✔___ 5. John had a streak of <u>misfortune</u> when he lost his wallet and had his bike stolen.

__✔___ 6. The <u>lofty</u> towers of the castle provided a wonderful view of the village below.

_____ 7. Mr. Mitchell has a <u>lofty</u> workshop in his basement.

__✔___ 8. The most <u>comely</u> boy in the class was chosen for the part of the handsome prince.

"East of the Sun and West of the Moon," *Landscapes* (Hardcover: pages 368-380) *Encounters* (Softcover: pages 104-116)

Objective: Use vocabulary words *(Comprehension and Vocabulary Skills)*

Extension: Have students write synonyms for *purpose, delectable,* and *lofty,* and antonyms for *comely* and *misfortune.*

102

Name _____ Date _____

A. Below are some statements about "East of the Sun and West of the Moon." Write **T** if the statement is true. Write **F** if it is false.

___F___ **1.** The woodcutter's daughter went with the White Bear for the sake of her family.

___F___ **2.** The girl refused to tell her family about her life at the shining castle.

___F___ **3.** The prince was glad the girl found out who he really was.

___F___ **4.** The girl was frightened when riding on the back of the North Wind.

___T___ **5.** The girl gave the golden apple to the troll in exchange for seeing the prince.

___T___ **6.** The troll princess was unable to wash out the drops of tallow in the prince's shirt.

___T___ **7.** The prince married the woodcutter's daughter, and they lived happily ever after.

B. Match each sentence beginning with an ending that will make a true statement about "East of the Sun and West of the Moon." Write the letter of the ending on the line.

___c___ **1.** The girl's mother

___d___ **2.** The prince

___a___ **3.** The woodcutter's daughter

___b___ **4.** An old woman

___f___ **5.** The troll

___e___ **6.** The North Wind

a. searched for the castle that lay east of the sun and west of the moon.

b. gave the girl a golden spinning wheel.

c. suggested that her daughter sneak into the White Bear's room.

d. was under a spell cast by a wicked troll.

e. took the girl to the castle.

f. flew into a rage and burst on the spot.

"East of the Sun and West of the Moon," *Landscapes* (Hardcover: pages 368-380) *Encounters* (Softcover: pages 104-116)

Objective: Demonstrate story comprehension *(Comprehension and Vocabulary Skills)*

Name _____   Date _____

Read the stories below. Then circle the letter next to the phrase that best completes each sentence.

Once long ago there lived a king named Midas. He ruled in a land called Phrygia. Midas loved gold and one day was allowed to make one wish by the god Dionysus. The king asked that everything he touch turn to gold. The god granted his wish. At first, Midas was pleased with his golden touch. But when he tried to eat or drink, the food and liquid turned to gold along with everything else he touched. Midas feared he would starve to death. He asked Dionysus to take back his golden touch. The god ordered him to go to a mountain stream and wash himself. The golden touch washed away from Midas and he became a sadder but wiser man.

1. The story takes place _____.
   a. long ago in Phrygia
   b. in the kingdom of Midas a few years ago
   c. today in Phrygia

2. The plot of the story involves _____.
   a. a king who loved gold
   b. a god who granted a king his wish
   c. a king who came to regret his wish of the golden touch

It was a glorious spring day. The wind whipped across the bright blue sky like a child at play. Harry raced outside carrying his new red kite and tossed it up into the air. The wind lifted the kite. Up, up, up it went into the heavens. Harry let out the string as he ran across the green meadow alive with wildflowers. The kite soared higher and higher until it was a speck of red against the sky. It was a day Harry would never forget.

3. The mood of the story is _____.
   a. sad   **b.** funny   **c.** joyful

4. The story is told from the point of view of _____.
   a. The author in the third person
   b. Harry in the first person
   c. Harry in the third person

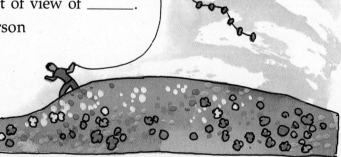

"East of the Sun and West of the Moon," *Landscapes* (Hardcover: pages 368-380) *Encounters* (Softcover: pages 104-116)

Objective: Identify plot, setting, mood, narrative point of view (*Literature and Language Skills*)

Extension: Have students describe the setting and plot of the second story.

104

Name

Date

A. Read the sentences. Then complete each sentence by circling the letter before each answer.

1. You would turn to a book's _____ if you were looking for other books that contained information on the same topic as the book you were reading.
   a. title page   b. index   c. glossary   (d.) bibliography

2. If you wanted to find information about a certain topic in a book, you would probably turn to the book's _____.
   a. title page   (b.) index   c. glossary   d. bibliography

3. A bibliography is arranged alphabetically according to _____.
   a. book title   (b.) author's last name
   c. publisher   d. city of publication

4. An index is arranged alphabetically according to _____.
   a. subheadings   b. page numbers
   c. book titles   (d.) topic headings

B. Read the bibliography entry below. Then match each numbered part with its description by writing the number of the part in the blank.

Barton, Nathaniel. Waves, Wind, and Weather. New York: David McKay, 1977					
(1)	(2)	(3)	(4)	(5)	(6)

___3___ **a.** title of book

___6___ **b.** year of publication

___2___ **c.** author's first name

___4___ **d.** city of publication

___1___ **e.** author's last name

___5___ **f.** name of publisher

"East of the Sun and West of the Moon," *Landscapes* **(Hardcover: pages 368-380)** *Encounters* **(Softcover: pages 104-116)**
Objective: Identify parts of a book: index, bibliography *(Study Skills)*   **Extension:** Have students choose topics from a textbook and locate information on the topics by using the book's index.

105

Name   Date

Read the definitions below. Then fill in the circle next to the word that is defined.

1. the outer surface or part
   - (a) exterior
   - (b) caution
   - (c) artificial

2. passing through or into, especially by force
   - (a) intercepted
   - (b) penetrating
   - (c) primitive

3. held in balance
   - (a) propose
   - (b) securely
   - (c) poised

4. bad luck
   - (a) misfortune
   - (b) misgivings
   - (c) penetrating

5. free time
   - (a) caution
   - (b) exterior
   - (c) leisure

6. firmly; tightly; in a stable way
   - (a) securely
   - (b) poised
   - (c) primitive

7. delicious
   - (a) comely
   - (b) delectable
   - (c) artificial

8. seized or stopped on the way
   - (a) intercepted
   - (b) penetrating
   - (c) poised

9. extending high in the air; towering
   - (a) comely
   - (b) exterior
   - (c) lofty

10. feelings of doubt or uneasiness
    - (a) caution
    - (b) misgivings
    - (c) misfortune

11. simple or crude
    - (a) moderate
    - (b) artificial
    - (c) primitive

12. kept within reasonable limits; not going to extremes
    - (a) misfortune
    - (b) moderate
    - (c) securely

13. pleasing in appearance; good-looking
    - (a) comely
    - (b) lofty
    - (c) securely

14. care with regard to danger or risk
    - (a) misfortune
    - (b) leisure
    - (c) caution

15. not natural; made by humans
    - (a) moderate
    - (b) artificial
    - (c) delectable

Cumulative Vocabulary Review

Objective: Use vocabulary words *(Comprehension and Vocabulary Skills)*

Extension: Have students choose six words from the page and write a sentence for each.

Name _____   Date _____

Read each paragraph. Then fill in the circle next to the best answer to each question.

Ken watched the fish swimming in the tank. He watched its sides puff in and out as its mouth opened and closed. Ken looked at his science book and read: "Water constantly moves in at a fish's mouth and out again through the gills. The gills are made of many tiny thin-walled blood vessels, which are always full of blood. After the water passes through the gills, some of the oxygen dissolved in it seeps into these blood vessels. At the same time, carbon dioxide seeps out of the vessels and into the water. In this way, the fish receives life-giving oxygen while freeing itself of carbon dioxide."

1. What happens after water passes through the gills?
   (a) Oxygen seeps into the blood vessels.
   (b) Water passes through the fish's mouth.
   (c) Carbon dioxide seeps into the water.
   (d) The blood vessels fill with blood.

2. What happens at the same time oxygen seeps into the blood vessels?
   (a) Water moves in at the fish's mouth.
   (b) Ken opens his book.
   (c) Carbon dioxide seeps into the water.
   (d) Water passes through the gills.

Leslie had to enter the canoe carefully to prevent it from overturning. She brought the canoe alongside the river's bank and, standing near the back end, faced the front of the canoe. Leslie took a deep breath, grasped the side of the canoe with one hand, and placed one foot into the canoe. She gingerly reached across and grabbed the far side of the canoe with her other hand as she shifted her weight onto the foot in the canoe. Then Leslie brought the other foot over the edge and sat down. She had done it!

3. What happened just after Leslie grasped the side of the canoe with one hand?
   (a) She paddled the canoe.   (b) She took a deep breath.
   (c) She shifted her weight.   (d) She placed a foot in the canoe.

4. What did Leslie do just before she sat down?
   (a) She stood near the back end of the canoe.
   (b) She brought the other foot into the canoe.
   (c) She grabbed the far side of the canoe.
   (d) She shifted her weight.

"Float Down the Tamarack," *Landscapes* (Hardcover: pages 402-413) *Forces* (Softcover: pages 10-21)

Objective: Identify sequence of events: explicit or implied
(Comprehension and Vocabulary Skills)

Extension: Have students list the events of one of the paragraphs on this page in sequential order.

Name _____ Date _____

A. Match each word on the left with its definition on the right. Write the letter of the definition on the line.

__d__ **1.** incredible

__c__ **2.** comparison

__e__ **3.** desperate

__a__ **4.** positioned

__b__ **5.** mishaps

a. put in a particular place

b. unfortunate accidents

c. the act of comparing in order to find likenesses or differences

d. hard or impossible to believe

e. ready or willing to take any risk

B. Read the story. Choose words from the box to finish the sentences. Write your answers on the numbered lines below the story.

| incredible | comparisons | desperate | positioned | mishaps |

Jean and John were twins. Because of this, it seemed that people were always making ___(1)___ between them. Both Jean and John felt that they were in constant competition.

One day, John became ___(2)___ to do something better than Jean. He decided the best way to do this would be to enter the fishing contest at Crawly's Creek. On the day of the contest, John ___(3)___ himself just downstream of Jean. He weighted his line and tossed it into the water just as Jean tossed hers. That's when a series of hilarious ___(4)___ began to occur.

John felt a tug on his line. Jean felt a tug on her line and began to reel it in. John's rod was bent over as if it would snap. Jean's was almost yanked out of her hands. John said he had an ___(5)___ fish on the line. Jean said hers was a monster. People ran over to watch the struggle. Suddenly, it was over. Jean and John stood facing each other sheepishly, their lines entangled and each had an incredible catch. They had caught each other.

1. _____comparisons_____ **2.** _____desperate_____

3. _____positioned_____ **4.** _____mishaps_____

5. _____incredible_____

"Float Down the Tamarack," *Landscapes* (Hardcover: pages 402-413) *Forces* (Softcover: pages 10-21)

Objective: Use vocabulary words *(Comprehension and Vocabulary Skills)*

Extension: Have students write a story using the words in the box in Part B.

Name   Date

Below are some questions about "Float Down the Tamarack." Write a complete sentence to answer each question. (Answers will vary.)

1. Why did Seth and Daniel find it impossible to paddle the canoe as they began their journey?

   The brush was too thick; the stream was too crooked and often too shallow. They had to push

   the canoe with the paddles. They had to lie in the canoe and pull themselves along.

2. After the boys reached the pond, why did they almost forget that they had come to fish?

   They were distracted by the wildlife and the natural beauty that surrounded them.

3. Why were Daniel and Seth disappointed to find dace on their lines?

   Dace is a food fish for trout that can be caught anywhere. Dace always got to the bait before

   other fish.

4. How did Daniel feel about Seth's catch? Why do you think that?

   Answers should include the author's mention of Daniel's jealousy. Daniel wished he had caught

   the fish and found it hard to be as excited about the catch as Seth was.

5. How do you think Seth felt about his catch? Why do you think that?

   Answers should include that Seth felt proud and pleased. He spoke about the struggle and the

   way the fish jumped. He talked to himself about the fish as he looked for wood.

6. If you were Daniel or Seth, would you go back to the beaver pond? Why or why not?

"Float Down the Tamarack," *Landscapes* (Hardcover: pages 402-413) *Forces* (Softcover: pages 10-21)
Objective: Demonstrate story comprehension *(Comprehension and Vocabulary Skills)*

Name _____   Date _____

A. Circle the letter next to the correct meaning of each numbered word.

1. uncertain
  a. less than certain
  b. completely certain
  (c.) not certain

2. misunderstand
  a. not understand
  (b.) understand wrongly
  c. understand correctly

3. nonviolent
  (a.) not violent
  b. relating to violence
  c. similar to violence

4. unpack
  a. pack again
  (b.) opposite of pack
  c. incorrectly packed

5. misinform
  a. inform correctly
  b. not inform
  (c.) inform wrongly

6. nonprofessional
  (a.) not professional
  b. very professional
  c. less than professional

7. unkind
  a. more than kind
  (b.) not kind
  c. always kind

8. misbehave
  a. behave well
  (b.) behave badly
  c. not behave

B. Add each prefix to the base word to form a new word. Then write the definition of the new word.

Prefix	Base Word	New Word	Definition
1. un-	lock	unlock	opposite of lock; open
2. non-	resident	nonresident	not a resident
3. mis-	represent	misrepresent	represent badly or wrongly
4. un-	important	unimportant	not important
5. non-	fiction	nonfiction	not fiction
6. mis-	match	mismatch	match wrongly
7. non-	metal	nonmetal	not metal
8. un-	aware	unaware	not aware

"Float Down the Tamarack," *Landscapes* (Hardcover: pages 402-413) *Forces* (Softcover: pages 10-21)

Objective: Identify prefixes: *mis-, non-, un-* (Decoding and Phonics Skills)

Extension: Have students add one of the prefixes *mis-, non-,* or *un-* to the following words: *label, flammable, tasted, willing, calculate, toxic, tamed.*

110

MACMILLAN PUBLISHING COMPANY

Name _____   Date _____

Read each paragraph. Then underline the best answer for each question.

Rivers that maintain a steady flow throughout the year are excellent sources of power. The water they carry can be used for irrigation and industry. Rugged mountain streams, such as those found in California, have irregular flows which make them undependable sources of power. During the rainy season, these mountain streams can become powerful, but during the drier seasons they are often reduced to trickles, with some drying up completely.

What is the main idea of this passage?

a. Rivers having a steady flow are excellent sources of power, while those with irregular flows are not.

b. During the rainy season, rugged mountain streams can become powerful.

c. During the dry season, mountain streams are often reduced to trickles.

d. Many rivers are excellent sources of power.

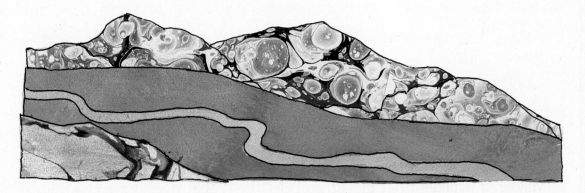

Lakes help keep the speed of many rivers constant. A lake tends to retain or store rainwater, even during the rainy seasons. It then releases the water at a constant rate to rivers that flow out of it. Lake Erie, for example, controls the speed of the Niagara River, which flows from it. The water that Lake Erie feeds to the Niagara River remains constant so that the speed of the river changes little from season to season.

What is the main idea of this passage?

a. Lake Erie controls the speed of the Niagara River.

b. The Niagara River flows out of Lake Erie.

c. Lakes keep the speed of many rivers constant by storing rainwater and releasing it at a constant rate.

d. The speed of the Niagara River changes little from season to season.

"The Changing River," *Landscapes* (Hardcover: pages 414-421) *Forces* (Softcover: pages 22-29)

Objective: Infer main idea: from two sentences (*Comprehension and Vocabulary Skills*)

Extension: Challenge students to write the main idea of the two paragraphs on this page.

Name _____   Date _____

A. Read each sentence. Choose a word from the box to complete the sentence. Write your answer on the line.

gradually	evidence	course	recedes	exposed

1. The flow of the river _____ gradually _____ smoothed its rocky banks.

2. Sometimes the water _____ recedes _____, leaving sediments behind.

3. Each year the Mississippi Delta shows more _____ evidence _____ of new growth.

4. The _____ course _____ of the river helps change the shape of the land.

5. When the river dries up, the river bed is _____ exposed _____.

B. Circle the letter next to the word that completes each sentence.

1. The _____ a river takes is often determined by the shape of the land through which it flows.

   a. evidence   **b.** gradually   **c.** course

2. The course of a river changes so _____ that it sometimes goes unnoticed for many years.

   a. gradually   **b.** exposed   **c.** evidence

3. Photographs taken from the air provide _____ that rivers have changed their course over a period of thousands of years.

   a. evidence   **b.** gradually   **c.** recedes

4. When the water _____ from the flood plains, it leaves rich minerals brought from farther up the river valley.

   a. exposed   **b.** recedes   **c.** gradually

5. The _____ slopes and rocks along a river's edge are further worn away by small streams, rain, and wind.

   a. evidence   **b.** gradually   **c.** exposed

Name   Date

A. Below are some statements about "The Changing River." Write **T** if the statement is true. Write **F** if the statement is false.

___T___ **1.** Spring is flood time for the river.

___F___ **2.** The Grand Canyon was carved by the Colorado River alone.

___T___ **3.** As a river slows, the sediment it carries settles to the river bottom.

___T___ **4.** In times of flood, areas covered by water are called flood plains.

___F___ **5.** The Mississippi flows into the Pacific Ocean with more than 700 million tons of sediment each year.

___F___ **6.** Each year the Mississippi Delta loses 300 feet to the Gulf.

___T___ **7.** A small stream behaves in a similar way to a big river.

___F___ **8.** Oxbow lakes are formed when a river takes a winding course.

B. Below are some questions about "The Changing River." Write a complete sentence to answer each question. (Answers will vary.)

1. Where do many rivers begin?

Many rivers begin in mountains or in hilly country.

2. What does the force of the water do in flood time?

The water loosens boulders and tumbles them. It smooths them to stones, then to pebbles, and eventually to grains of sand.

3. What happens to a river as time passes?

The water moves with less energy. It begins to cut sideways into a valley instead of down. The valley becomes U-shaped. The river changes course.

4. The Rio Grande is a river that makes up part of the international boundary between Mexico and the United States. How might this fact affect the southern border of the United States over time?

Answers will vary, but students should note that as the river changes, so does the boundary.

"**The Changing River,**" *Landscapes* **(Hardcover: pages 414-421)** *Forces* **(Softcover: pages 22-29)**
Objective: Demonstrate story comprehension *(Comprehension and Vocabulary Skills)*

Name _____ Date _____

Read each paragraph. Then use complete sentences to answer the questions.

The water cycle is an ongoing process that constantly replaces our water supply with water we have already used. This process begins with precipitation in the form of rain or snow. The precipitation seeps into the ground or falls directly into lakes, rivers, and oceans. At the same time, evaporation is occurring. Evaporation is caused by the sun's heat. The heat changes the water found on earth, including the water found in plants and animals, to water vapor. The water vapor is then carried back into the air where it is stored as clouds until it is released as precipitation.

1. What happens at the same time that precipitation is occurring?

   Evaporation is occurring. _____

   _____

2. What happens after the water vapor is carried back into the air?

   The water vapor is stored as clouds until it is released as precipitation. _____

   _____

Arlene packed another box of clothing and passed it up the attic ladder to her mother. There was a sudden crack of thunder and the baby began to cry. Arlene picked up the baby and hummed softly as she carried it to the window. The river had risen considerably, running up the walkway and lapping at the front steps. A barn door floated across what had once been the front lawn. Arlene wiped a tear from her own eyes. All they could do was move their belongings up and wait for the rescue boats to take them to safety.

3. What happened just before the baby began to cry?

   There was a sudden crack of thunder. _____

   _____

4. What happened just after Arlene walked to the window?

   A barn door drifted across the lawn. _____

   _____

MACMILLAN PUBLISHING COMPANY

"The Changing River," *Landscapes* (Hardcover: pages 414-421) *Forces* (Softcover: pages 22-29)

Objective: Identify sequence of events: explicit or implied
(Comprehension and Vocabulary Skills)

Extension: Have students draw and label a picture of the events in the first paragaph on this page.

114

Name   Date

Read each set of directions. Where would you be if you follow the directions? Fill in the circle next to the answer.

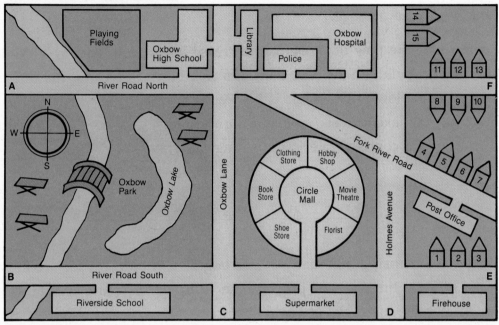

1. Start at point A. Go east on River Road North until you reach the first intersection. Then go south. At the next intersection, go east. The building on the southern side of the street is _____.
   - (a) the supermarket
   - (b) the firehouse
   - (c) Riverside School
   - (d) Circle Mall

2. Start at point D. Go north on Holmes Avenue. At the third intersection, go east. The address of the second house on the northern side of the street is _____.
   - (a) 5 Fork River Road
   - (b) 13 River Road North
   - (c) 12 River Road North
   - (d) 14 Holmes Avenue

3. Start at point C. Go north. Then at the first intersection, go west for half a block. On the northern side of the street, you will see _____.
   - (a) Riverside School
   - (b) Oxbow Lake
   - (c) picnic tables
   - (d) playing fields

4. Start at point E. Go west. At the first intersection, go north until you reach the next intersection, then go west. Halfway down the block on the southern side of the street is _____.
   - (a) the supermarket
   - (b) Oxbow Hospital
   - (c) the firehouse
   - (d) Circle Mall

"The Changing River," *Landscapes* (Hardcover: pages 414-421) *Forces* (Softcover: pages 22-29)

Objective: Follow multistep directions (*Comprehension and Vocabulary Skills*)

Extension: Have students write the directions for the shortest route from the fire house to the playing fields.

Name   Date

Read each paragraph. Underline the two sentences that make up the main idea of the paragraph. Then write the sentences as a single main idea statement on the line below the passage.

1. Regulating the flow of a river can increase its value. One way in which to do this is to build a dam. The dam acts as a barrier blocking the flow of the water. As the flow of the water is blocked, a lake or reservoir is formed behind the dam. The lake collects water during the rainy season. The dam can release this water at a constant rate, even during dry spells.

Sample answer: One way in which to regulate the flow of a river is to build a dam.

_____

2. It is not surprising that many of our largest and oldest cities are found along rivers. In early times, rivers provided an easy source of transportation and quickly became highways of travel and trade. They provided power to run mills and factories, as well as supplying people with fish and a source of recreation. Today, rivers are still used for the same reasons. In fact, the varied uses of a river have influenced the growth of many countries as well as cities.

Sample answer: Because of a river's varied uses, many cities have grown along rivers.

_____

3. Valuable ground water helps to keep the surface waters—and the vegetation that depends upon them—from drying up. Ground water usually comes to the earth's surface in springs, marshes, ponds, lakes, and rivers. In a few places, this water is located too deep within the ground to be of much use. However, in most regions, where it doesn't reach the surface, ground water lies within fifty feet of the surface. Thus it can easily be reached by wells. This is true of almost every land surface on earth.

Sample answer: Almost every land surface on earth has valuable ground water beneath it.

_____

Skills Activity, Main Idea, *Landscapes* **(Hardcover: pages 424-425)** *Forces* **(Softcover: pages 32-33)**

Objective: Infer main idea: from two sentences (*Comprehension and Vocabulary Skills*)

Extension: Have students write a paragraph using the following sentence as the main idea: Lakes are a source of recreation for people of all ages.

116

Name _____ Date _____

Read the story. Then correctly complete the sentences below by writing **before, after,** or **as** in the blanks.

When he went out to work in his cornfield on February 20, 1943, Mexican farmer Dionisio Pulido was startled to find that an 80-foot-long crack had opened in the land during the night. As Pulido and his family looked on in awe, ash and red-hot stones burst from the opening. The Pulidos were watching the birth of a volcano.

Pulido raced to the village to report what had happened. Soon, dozens of geologists were studying the sight. The volcano grew with amazing speed. It was 550 feet high by the end of the week. As the volcano continued to grow, it poured out huge amounts of lava and ash, destroying Pulido's cornfield. Nine years after its beginning, the volcano fell silent. Its final height was 1,353 feet.

1. An 80-foot-long crack had opened in the land _____ before _____ Pulido went out to his cornfield on Feburary 20, 1943.

2. Ash and red-hot stones burst from the opening _____ as _____ Pulido and his family looked on in awe.

3. Pulido raced to the village _____ after _____ he watched the birth of the volcano.

4. Dozens of geologists went to the site _____ after _____ Pulido reported what had happened.

5. The volcano poured out lava and ash _____ as _____ it continued to grow.

6. Pulido's cornfield was destroyed _____ before _____ the volcano reached its full height.

7. The volcano fell silent _____ after _____ it reached a height of 1,353 feet.

"The Big Wave," *Landscapes* **(Hardcover: pages 426-439)** *Forces* **(Softcover: pages 34-47)**

Objective: Identify sequence of events: explicit or implied
(Comprehension and Vocabulary Skills)

Extension: Have students write five events in sequential order numbering each event.

Name _____   Date _____

A. Match each word on the left with its definition on the right. Write the letter of the definition on the line.

___b___ **1.** ancient

___c___ **2.** generation

___d___ **3.** falter

___e___ **4.** urgently

___a___ **5.** unconscious

a. temporarily unable to sense things

b. very old

c. a group of people born about the same time

d. to act with hesitation or uncertainty

e. insistently; pleadingly

B. Read each sentence below. Write **Yes** if the underlined vocabulary word is used correctly. Write **No** if it is not used correctly.

___Yes___ **1.** A whole <u>generation</u> of children had grown since the last tidal wave.

___Yes___ **2.** The people paid little attention to the bell whose ring was <u>urgently</u> warning them to leave the village.

___No___ **3.** Amy's family heard the bell and began to <u>falter</u> because they were sure of the danger as they rushed up the <u>hill</u> as fast as they could go.

___Yes___ **4.** The huge wave destroyed much of the village and the <u>ancient</u> sea wall that had protected it for hundreds of years.

___No___ **5.** Several people who had witnessed the disaster ran down the hill <u>unconscious</u>.

___No___ **6.** The <u>ancient</u> schoolhouse, built two years ago, was still standing and being used as a makeshift hospital.

___Yes___ **7.** Amy was <u>unconscious</u> when her parents carried her to the schoolhouse.

___No___ **8.** They <u>urgently</u> asked the doctor to ignore Amy.

"The Big Wave," *Landscapes* (Hardcover: pages 426-439) *Forces* (Softcover: pages 34-47)

Objective: Use vocabulary words *(Comprehension and Vocabulary Skills)*

Extension: Have students rewrite the sentences marked NO in Part B, so that the underlined words are used correctly.

118

Name _____ Date _____

Below are some questions about "The Big Wave. "Write a complete sentence to answer each question. (Answers will vary.)

1. What did Kino and his father do on the morning of the Big Wave?

They watched the sky and the sea.

_____

2. What did Kino's mother do on the morning of the Big Wave?

She took down everything that could fall or be broken; she packed the good dishes

in straw.

3. Who raised the red flag, and what did it mean?

The Old Gentleman raised the red flag to warn the people to be ready for whatever

happened.

4. What message did the tolling of the bell send the people?

The bell called the villagers to come and take shelter within the walls of the Old

Gentleman's castle.

5. How did Kino signal to Jiya that he wanted him to come?

Kino took off his white girdle cloth; using both hands, he waved it high above

his head.

6. Do you think the people of the village respected the Old Gentlemen? Why or why not?

Answers will vary but students should note that they must have respected the Old Gentleman

because they acknowledged his flag and the tolling of his bell.

_____

7. Why do you think the houses in the village had no windows that faced the sea?

_____

_____

"The Big Wave," *Landscapes* **(Hardcover: pages 426-439)** *Forces* **(Softcover: pages 34-47)**

Objective: Demonstrate story comprehension *(Comprehension and Vocabulary Skills)*

119

Name _____   Date _____

Study the graphs below. Then circle the letter next to the answer to each question.

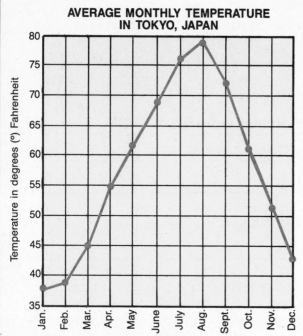

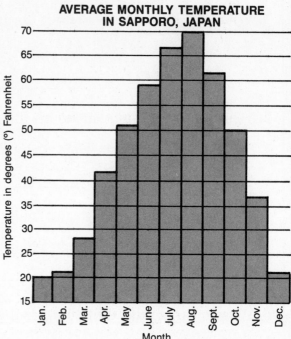

1. What is the hottest month in Tokyo and Sapporo?

    a. June   **b.** July   **c.** August   **d.** September

2. In what month is the average temperature in Sapporo 50°?

    a. April   **b.** May   **c.** September   **d.** October

3. About how many degrees difference is there between the hottest and coldest months in Tokyo?

    a. 20°   **b.** 30°   **c.** 40°   **d.** 50°

4. During which two months is the average temperature in Sapporo exactly the same?

    a. January and December   **b.** February and December

    c. May and October   **d.** July and August

5. How many degrees colder is Sapporo than Tokyo in March?

    a. 17°   **b.** 10°   **c.** 13°   **d.** 23°

6. Between which two months does the average monthly temperature in Tokyo and Sapporo increase the most?

    a. April and May   **b.** March and April

    c. June and July   **d.** November and December

"The Big Wave," *Landscapes* (Hardcover: pages 426-443) *Forces* (Softcover: pages 50-51)

Objective: Interpret graphic aids: graphs (bar, line) *(Study Skills)*   **Extension:** Have students plot a line graph using the information in the bar graph on this page.

Name _____ Date _____

Study the line and bar graphs below. Then fill in the circle next to the answer for each question.

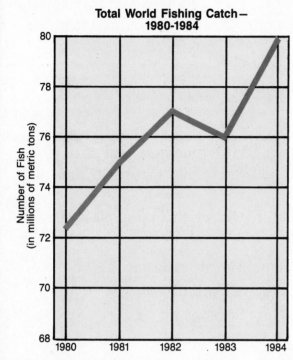

Total World Fishing Catch— 1980-1984

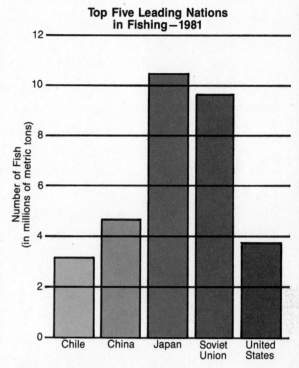

Top Five Leading Nations in Fishing—1981

1. Which nation leads the world in the number of fish it catches?
   - (a) Chile
   - (b) China
   - **(c) Japan**
   - (d) Soviet Union

2. How many metric tons of fish were caught in 1983?
   - (a) 75,000,000
   - **(b) 76,000,000**
   - (c) 80,000,000
   - (d) 72,300,000

3. The total number of metric tons of fish caught has increased every year except one. In which year did the total number of fish caught decrease?
   - (a) 1980
   - (b) 1981
   - (c) 1982
   - **(d) 1983**

4. How many metric tons of fish did the Soviet Union catch in 1981?
   - **(a) 9,500,000**
   - (b) 10,500,000
   - (c) 8,500,000
   - (d) 4,500,000

5. Of the five leading fishing nations, which country caught the least metric tonnage of fish in 1981?
   - **(a) Chile**
   - (b) China
   - (c) Japan
   - (d) United States

6. How many metric tons of fish did the United States catch in 1981?
   - (a) 4,500,000
   - (b) 2,000,000
   - (c) 4,000,000
   - **(d) 3,500,000**

7. In what year was the total world's catch equal to 75,000,000 metric tons?
   - (a) 1980
   - **(b) 1981**
   - (c) 1982
   - (d) 1983

Skills Activity, Graphs, *Landscapes* (Hardcover: pages 442-443) *Forces* (Softcover: pages 50-51)

Objective: Interpret graphic aids: graphs (bar, line) *(Study Skills)*   **Extension:** Have students write a paragraph describing the information in the line graph.

Name _____   Date _____

Read each paragraph. Then underline the best answer for each question.

When the Johnsons planned their vacation, they had been told they had the last campsite available. Imagine their surprise when they found out that they were the *only* campers.

"Where is everyone?" asked Mr. Johnson.

"The scientists and their volcano scared them away," answered the old campground owner.

"Volcano!" exclaimed Ben and Emily.

"Don't worry," said the owner. "I've been on this mountain over sixty years, and there's never been an eruption. Oh, no! Here comes that pesky park ranger again!"

"Excuse me, folks," said the ranger, "but the geologists up the mountain want me to ask all campers to vacate the area."

1. Who is best qualified to state an opinion about the volcano?

   a. Mr. Johnson   b. the park ranger

   c. the old man   d. the geologists

2. What do you think the Johnson family should do?

   a. enjoy the vacation they had planned

   b. find another campsite off the mountain

   c. stay until the volcano begins to erupt

   d. go back home and plan another vacation

Ginny was writing a report on a local volcano. She wanted to know what happened the last time it erupted. Ginny asked her parents, but they said the last eruption took place sixty-three years ago, long before they were born. Her mother suggested visiting the retirement village and seeing if any of the residents remembered the last eruption. Her father suggested checking the library for old town newspapers that might have eye-witness accounts and pictures. Her brother told her to look for pictures in the encyclopedia.

3. Where would Ginny find the most accurate account of the volcano's last eruption?

   a. from her parents   b. from old town papers

   c. from elderly people   d. from encyclopedias

"Why Mount St. Helens Blew Its Top," *Landscapes* **(Hardcover: pages 444-453)** *Forces* **(Softcover: pages 52-61)**

Objective: Evaluate and make judgments *(Comprehension and Vocabulary Skills)*

Extension: Have students explain why the other choices on this page are not good value judgments.

Name   Date

A. Circle the letter of the word that best completes each sentence.

1. A _____ studies the earth's structure.
   (i.) geologist   **j.** pressure   **k.** crater

2. Forces exerted by one thing upon another are called _____.
   r. crater   **s.** expands   **(t.)** pressures

3. When something _____, it becomes larger in size.
   a. crater   **(b.)** expands   **c.** pressures

4. A _____ is a bowl-shaped hollow area at the mouth of a volcano.
   j. erupt   **k.** geologist   **(l.)** crater

5. To shoot forth lava, as a volcano does, is to _____.
   (e.) erupt   **f.** geologist   **g.** crater

6. The pilot flew over the volcano so we could see into its _____.
   v. erupt   **(w.)** crater   **x.** pressures

7. The _____ told us about the history of the volcano.
   (i.) geologist   **j.** pressure   **k.** crater

8. A volcano erupts when _____ build up under the earth's surface.
   r. crater   **s.** expands   **(t.)** pressures

9. A volcano _____ before it erupts.
   r. crater   **(s.)** expands   **t.** pressures

10. A volcano's _____ is usually larger after an eruption.
    (t.) crater   **u.** geologist   **v.** erupt

11. No one can predict exactly when a volcano will _____.
    (o.) erupt   **p.** geologist   **q.** crater

12. Each new eruption helps a _____ learn more about volcanos.
    o. erupt   **(p.)** geologist   **q.** crater

B. Write the letters you circled on the lines to answer the riddle. How did the volcano show its anger?

$\frac{i}{1} \frac{t}{2} \quad \frac{b}{3} \frac{l}{4} \frac{e}{5} \frac{w}{6} \quad \frac{i}{7} \frac{t}{8} \frac{s}{9} \quad \frac{t}{10} \frac{o}{11} \frac{p}{12}$

"Why Mount St. Helens Blew Its Top," *Landscapes* (Hardcover: **pages 444-452**) *Forces* (Softcover: **pages 52-61**)

Objective: Use vocabulary words *(Comprehension and Vocabulary Skills)*

Extension: Have students define the following words: *geologist, pressures, expands, crater, erupt.*

Name _____ Date _____

A. Below are some sentences about "Why Mount St. Helens Blew Its Top."
Write **T** if the statement is true. Write **F** if it is false.

___F___ **1.** Mount St. Helens is a volcano located in Florida.

___F___ **2.** The eruption of Mount St. Helens came as no surprise to most
Americans.

___T___ **3.** The earth's crust is made up of plates that look similar to the cracked
ice on ponds.

___T___ **4.** The earth's mantle is never still.

___F___ **5.** Deep within the earth is a mixture of melted rock and ice called
magma.

___T___ **6.** Magma forces its way to the surface when it is pushed by pressures in
the mantle and crust.

___T___ **7.** Magma that reaches the surface of the earth is called lava.

___F___ **8.** The lava from a volcano never cools or hardens.

___F___ **9.** It is unlikely that Mount St. Helens will ever erupt again.

B. Read each event below. Number the events in the order in which
they happened.

___4___ The volcano shook and spit in preparation for its 1980 eruption for two
months.

___1___ The Juan de Fuca plate pushed under the North American plate, helping
to form the Cascade Mountains.

___5___ Geologists measured the growth of a bulge on the north side of Mount
St. Helens.

___2___ Eruptions occurred in Mount St. Helens in 1857.

___6___ Mount St. Helens erupted on the morning of May 18, 1980.

___7___ COBBLESTONE magazine asked readers living near Mount St. Helens to
describe what the eruption was like.

___3___ Geologists warned that Mount St. Helens would erupt before the end of
the century.

MACMILLAN PUBLISHING COMPANY

"Why Mount St. Helens Blew Its Top," *Landscapes* **(Hardcover: pages 444-453)** *Forces* **(Softcover: pages 52-61)**
Objective: Demonstrate story comprehension *(Comprehension and*
Vocabulary Skills)
124

Name _____ Date _____

Study the diagram below. Fill in the circle next to the answer.

HOW MOVING TECTONIC PLATES MIGHT INTERACT

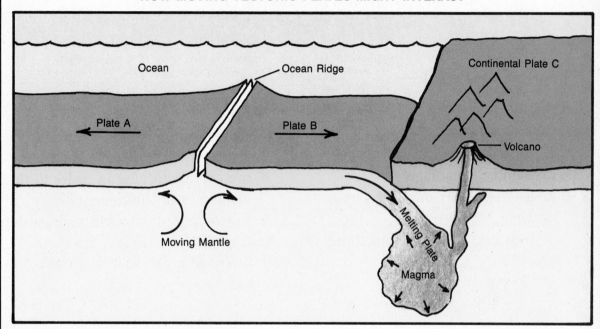

1. What happens as Plate B moves toward Plate C?
   - (a) Plate B is pushed over Plate C.
   - **(b)** Plate B is pushed under Plate C.
   - (c) Plate B surfaces above the ocean.
   - (d) Plate B collides with Plate A.

2. What is formed along the edge of Plate A and Plate B?
   - **(a)** a ridge
   - (b) Plate C
   - (c) a volcano
   - (d) a trench

3. What happens to Plate B as it is pushed under Plate C?
   - (a) It expands.
   - (b) It stops moving.
   - **(c)** It melts.
   - (d) It moves faster.

4. What is the material that results from the melting called?
   - (a) mantle
   - **(b)** magma
   - (c) volcano
   - (d) ridge

5. How might the pressure that builds up as a result of the melting process be released?
   - **(a)** through a volcanic eruption
   - (b) through the melting of the plates
   - (c) through the moving of the mantle
   - (d) through the creation of a trench

"Why Mount St. Helens Blew Its Top," *Landscapes* **(Hardcover: pages 444-453)** *Forces* **(Softcover: pages 52-61)**

Objective: Interpret graphic aids: diagrams *(Study Skills)*   **Extension:** Ask students to find out what else can happen as tectonic plates move forward and away from each other.

Name _____ Date _____

Use the words in the box and the clues below to complete the puzzle.

erupt	exposed	urgently	incredible
course	geologist	comparison	pressures
positioned	generation	expands	unconscious

ACROSS
1. hard to believe
2. left open; uncovered
3. insistently; pleadingly
4. forces exerted by one thing upon another
5. path or line in which something moves
6. put in a particular place

DOWN
2. makes larger in size; enlarges
7. unable to sense things
8. the act of studying in order to find likenesses or differences
9. to suddenly throw forth something
10. scientist who studies the earth
11. group of individuals born about the same time

Cumulative Vocabulary Review, *Landscapes* **(Hardcover: pages 444-453)** *Forces* **(Softcover: pages 52-61)**

Objective: Use vocabulary words *(Comprehension and Vocabulary Skills)*

Extension: Have students use ten of the vocabulary words in sentences.

126

MACMILLAN PUBLISHING COMPANY

Name _____ Date _____

A. Study the prefixes and their meanings in the box below. Then match each word on the left with its definition on the right. Write your answer on the line.

centi-	a hundred, a hundredth
deca-, deka-	ten
deci-	a tenth
kilo-	a thousand
milli-	a thousandth

_____d_____ **1.** cent   **a.** fraction with a denominator of ten

_____e_____ **2.** decade   **b.** unit of weight equalling 1000 tons

_____b_____ **3.** kiloton   **c.** one thousandth of a liter

_____c_____ **4.** milliliter   **d.** one hundredth part of a dollar

_____a_____ **5.** decimal   **e.** a period of ten years

B. Use your knowledge of prefixes and the clues below to solve the puzzles.

1. one thousand grams _kilogram_____

2. number of legs on a centipede _one hundred_____

3. an octagon has eight sides; a hexagon has six sides; and a _____decagon_____ has ten sides.

4. number of events in a decathlon _ten_____

5. number of watts in a kilowatt _a thousand watts_____

6. number of years in half a century _fifty_____

7. one-thousandth of a gram _milligram_____

8. one-hundredth of a gram _centigram_____

Skills Activity: Prefixes, *Landscapes* (Hardcover: pages 456-457) *Forces* (Softcover: pages 64-65)

Objective: Identify prefixes: *centi-, deca-, deka-, deci-, kilo-, milli-* (Decoding and Phonics Skills)   **Extension:** Have students use the words in Part A in sentences.

127

Name _____   Date _____

Read each sentence. Use context clues to figure out the meaning of the underlined word. Fill in the circle next to the meaning.

1. Mark was sorry he had <u>squandered</u> his allowance on video games.
   - (a) forgotten
   - **(b) foolishly spent**
   - (c) cleverly won
   - (d) earned

2. Naomi posted pictures of her lost cat in the <u>vicinity</u> of her home and school.
   - **(a) area near**
   - (b) backyard
   - (c) living room
   - (d) classroom

3. The Lyons family thoroughly enjoyed their weekend <u>junket</u> to the countryside.
   - (a) cruise
   - (b) meeting
   - (c) cleaning
   - **(d) trip**

4. One of Ben Franklin's most famous <u>adages</u> is "A penny saved is a penny earned."
   - (a) paintings
   - **(b) sayings**
   - (c) rock songs
   - (d) poems

5. The <u>indelible</u> ink left a spot on my shirt that won't wash out.
   - (a) invisible
   - (b) washable
   - (c) stain
   - **(d) permanent**

6. Good food, fresh air, and daily exercise will keep you feeling <u>robust</u>.
   - (a) sickly
   - **(b) healthy**
   - (c) sore
   - (d) grumpy

7. Scraping and sanding the paint off the old shutters was a <u>tedious</u> job that no one wanted.
   - **(a) boring**
   - (b) unusual
   - (c) amusing
   - (d) interesting

8. It is <u>mandatory</u> for all people traveling out of the country to have a passport to prove their citizenship.
   - (a) senseless
   - **(b) necessary**
   - (c) recommended
   - (d) useless

9. The words *level, radar, bib,* and *pop* are examples of <u>palindromes</u>.
   - (a) words that have two or more syllables
   - (b) words that have one short and one long vowel
   - **(c) words that read the same forwards and backwards**
   - (d) words that are made up of only one syllable

10. Andrea decided to pick a <u>posy</u> from the garden and place it in a vase on the dinner table.
    - **(a) bouquet of flowers**
    - (b) lettuce
    - (c) vegetables
    - (d) fruit

"A Strange Sled Race," *Landscapes* (Hardcover: pages 458-465) *Forces* (Softcover: pages 66-73)

Objective: Define words using context clues *(Comprehension and Vocabulary Skills)*

Extension: Have students demonstrate their understanding of the underlined words by having them use the words in sentences.

128

Name   Date

A. Match each word with its definition. Write the letter of the definition on the line.

___b___ **1.** myth   **a.** to resist boldly and openly

___e___ **2.** inferior   **b.** story that expresses a belief

___c___ **3.** dwindled   **c.** became gradually smaller or less

___a___ **4.** defy   **d.** melted by heat

___f___ **5.** garments   **e.** of poor quality; below average

___d___ **6.** molten   **f.** articles of clothing

B. Read the story. Choose words from the box to complete the sentences. Write your answers on the numbered lines below the story.

defy	**dwindled**	**garments**	**inferior**	**molten**	**myth**

Ben decided to write a __(1)__ that would explain why the volcano Haleakala in Hawaii was no longer active. He wrote:

One day Volcano Goddess put on her fiery __(2)__ and went in search of a new home. The mountain she favored was on the island of Maui. "This is where I will make my home," she announced. "I will name the place Haleakala: 'house of the sun.'"

Now Sun God became angry upon hearing this. "You must change the name of your home," he ordered.

"Why? The heat from my fires are not __(3)__ to yours."

Sun God looked with surprise at the goddess who dared __(4)__ him. "Then we will have a contest," he said. "Whichever of us can heat more of the world shall win."

Sun God shone brightly as Haleakala threw forth __(5)__ rock. Lava continued to flow from Haleakala, but it __(6)__ as it reached the sea. Sun God had won, and Volcano Goddess left Haleakala never to return.

1. _____myth_____   **2.** _____garments_____

3. _____inferior_____   **4.** _____defy_____

5. _____molten_____   **6.** _____dwindled_____

"A Strange Sled Race," *Landscapes* (Hardcover: pages 458-465) *Forces* (Softcover: pages 66-73)

Objective: Use vocabulary words (*Comprehension and Vocabulary Skills*)

Extension: Have students write a story using the words in the box in Part B.

Name _____   Date _____

A. The sentences below tell about "A Strange Sled Race," but they are not written in order. Number the events. The first event has been numbered for you.

_6_   **1.** The stranger stamped her foot and a large crack opened in the mountain.

_5_   **2.** The stranger demanded that Snow Goddess go first.

_7_   **3.** The snow maidens realized the stranger was Pele, Volcano Goddess.

_10_   **4.** Volcano Goddess was defeated and never crossed over to Poliahu's side of the mountain again.

_9_   **5.** Snow Goddess sent snow to cool Pele's fires.

_3_   **6.** A snow maiden offered a sled to the stranger.

_2_   **7.** A stranger appeared and challenged Poliahu to a contest.

_4_   **8.** The Snow Goddess beat the stranger at sledding twice.

_8_   **9.** Poliahu stood to face the fires of Pele.

_1_   **10.** Poliahu and her snow maidens were sledding.

B. The clothes of both Polaihu and Pele change with the mood of "The Strange Sled Race." Use complete sentences to describe and explain these changes. (Answers will vary.)

Polaihu When Polaihu is having fun and sled racing with her snow maidens, she is wearing a golden mantle, or cloak. When she goes through the wall of fire, her golden mantle catches fire, and she throws it off and was clothed in a dazzling white robe showing that she would be victorious.

Pele Pele was wearing a black robe which shows she was wicked or evil. When she tried to create a volcano, her robe turned to red to show the anger she felt. When she was defeated, her red mantle turned black again.

MACMILLAN PUBLISHING COMPANY

Name _____ Date _____

Read the paragraph. Then write a complete sentence to answer each question.

The snow maidens decided to have a party for Poliahu in honor of her bravery and success. They formed three committees to plan the party: Food, Decorations, and Entertainment.

A maiden on the food committee suggested they serve pineapple because that was her personal favorite. A second said that Poliahu had once thrown out some pineapple and probably didn't like it. A third reminded them that Poliahu had always wanted to attend a Hawaiian luau, or feast. The committee agreed to this idea and hurried to ask the village women what they should do.

The decorations committee quickly decided on a theme. To show that Pele would never return to their side of the mountain, they would decorate half the hall in silver (to stand for cool Poliahua) and the other half of the hall in gold (for the fiery Pele).

The entertainment committee wanted a band, but it was pointed out that the music Poliahu truly loved was laughter. One maiden proposed a storyteller since Poliahu loved stories. A second suggested a hula dancer because Poliahu loved dance. The maidens were trying to choose between these two ideas when it was suggested that they invent a hula dance that told the story of the strange sled race!

1. Why did the food committee decide to have a Hawaiian luau?

A luau was something that Poliahu had always wanted to attend.

2. Was the maiden correct in saying Poliahu didn't like pineapple? Why or why not?

No. Poliahu might have thrown out the pineapple for another reason. For example, it might

have been too ripe or even rotten.

3. Was the decorations committee's theme a good one? Why?

Answers may vary, but students should note that the committee kept to the idea of honoring

Poliahu.

4. Why did the entertainment committee decide to invent a hula dance?

They could then combine the two things that Poliahu loved: stories and dance.

"A Strange Sled Race," *Landscapes* (Hardcover: pages 458-465) *Forces* (Softcover: pages 66-73)

Objective: Evaluate and make judgments *(Comprehension and Vocabulary Skills)*

Extension: Have students write a paragraph explaining how Poliahu felt when she arrived at the party.

Name _____ Date _____

Read each sentence. Then write the event that happened first. If the events happened at the same time, write both events.

1. "Hold on!" Kim called as the ground began to shake.

   The ground began to shake. Kim called, "Hold on!"

2. Dennis peered into the large hole that Kim had fallen into.

   Kim fell into a large hole.

3. Dennis felt better after he heard Kim's voice.

   Dennis heard Kim's voice.

4. Kim had dusted herself off before she called to Dennis.

   Kim dusted herself off.

5. Kim turned quickly when she heard a strange noise behind her.

   Kim heard a strange noise.

6. As the carriage approached, Kim saw a boy leaning out the window.

   The carriage approached. Kim saw a boy leaning out the window.

7. The boy jumped from the carriage after it stopped.

   The carriage stopped.

8. Dennis slid down the embankment and landed at Kim's feet.

   Dennis slid down the embankment.

9. "You look like twins!" Kim explained as she looked at Dennis and the boy.

   Kim looked at each boy. She said they looked like twins.

10. "You're in the land of mirrors," the boy answered in response to Dennis's question.

    Dennis asked a question.

11. A girl got out of the carriage after the boy spoke.

    The boy spoke.

12. Before the girl could speak, Kim said, "Why, you look like me!"

    Kim said, "Why, you look like me!"

"Dorothy's Journey to the Center of the Earth," *Landscapes* (Hardcover: pages 466-480) *Forces* (Softcover: pages 74-88)

Objective: Identify sequence of events: explicit or implied *(Comprehension and Vocabulary Skills)*

Extension: Have students rewrite each sentence so that the events are stated in the order in which they happened.

Name _____   Date _____

A. Read each sentence. Then circle the letter of the word that best completes it.

1. Dorothy had been on many adventures and felt _____ to Zeb in that he had never been on an adventure before.
   a. authority   **(b.)** superior   **c.** suspended

2. "The shiny balls that are _____ in the air," Dorothy explained, "are probably this world's suns."
   a. authority   **b.** superior   **(c.)** suspended

3. A _____ of townspeople came marching towards Dorothy and Zeb.
   (a.) procession   **b.** exalted   **c.** suspended

4. "The person leading the parade must be someone of _____," Zeb whispered.
   a. exalted   **(b.)** authority   **c.** procession

5. The leader said that the people had decided to wait for their _____ ruler to decide what to do with the visitors.
   (a.) exalted   **b.** authority   **c.** procession

B. Write each word from the box on the blanks next to its definition. Then use the numbers under the letters to discover who you will read about in the next story.

suspended	superior	exalted	procession	authority

1. the power or right to command a u t h o r i t y
                  5 1   11

2. raised in rank or position e x a l t e d
        2   3 6

3. higher in rank or importance s u p e r i o r
                 12   4

4. hanging down from above s u s p e n d e d
        8   15   7

5. a ceremonious parade p r o c e s s i o n
        10   14   9   13

   h e a r t l e s s   p r i n c e
   1 2 3 4 5 6 7 8 9   10 11 12 13 14 15

"Dorothy's Journey to the Center of the Earth," *Landscapes* **(Hardcover: pages 466-480)** *Forces* **(Softcover: pages 74-88)**

Objective: Use vocabulary words *(Comprehension and Vocabulary Skills)*

Extension: Have students use the dictionary to write words related to *suspended, procession,* and *authority.*

133

Name _____   Date _____

A. Each quotation in the left column is from "Dorothy's Journey to the Center of the Earth." Match the quotation with the character on the right. Write the letter of your answer on the line.

___c___ **1.** "I can't explain why I happened to speak then."

___b___ **2.** "We'll never get home again, though!"

___e___ **3.** "I have nine lives."

___f___ **4.** "Tell me, intruder, was it you who caused the Rain of Stones?"

___a___ **5.** "Suppose we pick the Royal Princess."

___d___ **6.** "Give me the Star of Royalty!"

a. Dorothy
b. Zeb
c. Jim
d. the Princess
e. Eureka
f. the Prince

B. Below are some characters from "Dorothy's Journey to the Center of the Earth." Use complete sentences to describe each character. (Answers will vary.)

Dorothy Dorothy is the main character. She is used to having adventures, so she isn't afraid of the journey to the center of the earth and isn't worried about getting home again. She likes walking through the air, and is curious about the Mangaboos. It is her idea to pick the Royal Princess.

Zeb Zeb is Dorothy's cousin. He is more worried than Dorothy about getting home, but he, too, is curious. He is not as knowledgeable as Dorothy about things such as earthquakes, but he is a full partner in their adventure.

the Prince The Prince is the ruler of the Mangaboos. He is angry about the Rain of Stones and wants to hold Dorothy and Zeb responsible. In his selfishness and desire to continue his rule, the Prince leaves the Princess on the bush.

the Mangaboos The Mangaboos are unusual creatures living in a city of glass. Their faces are expressionless. They grow in folk gardens fully clothed attached to bushes. The Mangaboos are not picked until grown; that is why there are no children in the streets. The Mangaboos formed a procession and escorted the Princess to her palace.

MACMILLAN PUBLISHING COMPANY

"Dorothy's Journey to the Center of the Earth," *Landscapes* **(Hardcover: pages 466-480)** *Forces* **(Softcover: pages 74-88)**
Objective: Demonstrate story comprehension *(Comprehension and Vocabulary Skills)*

Name _____   Date _____

Imagine that your local library has asked its readers to complete a questionnaire. Read the form carefully. Then fill it out. (Answers will vary.)

Name _____
       last   first   middle initial

Address _____
        number   street

_____
       city   state   zip code

Phone _____ Age _____ Male _____ Female _____

How many books a month do you read? _____

Number the following types of books according to your interests. Use each number only once.

1=greatest interest   12=least interest

_____ biography   _____ folk tale   _____ realistic fiction

_____ mystery   _____ history   _____ poetry

_____ fantasy   _____ science   _____ geography

_____ science fiction   _____ how-to   _____ sports

List other types of books in order of preference.

_____

_____

What is your favorite book? Describe why it is your favorite in a few sentences.

_____

_____

_____

_____

"Dorothy's Journey to the Center of the Earth," *Landscapes* **(Hardcover: pages 466-480)** *Forces* **(Softcover: pages 74-88)**

Objective: Follow multistep directions *(Study Skills)*

Extension: Have students write two questions to add to the questionnaire on this page. Then have them answer their questions.

Name _____ Date _____

Read the paragraph. Then write a complete sentence to answer each question.

Henry, Craig, and Marta were lost. They had stopped to examine a shallow underground stream and didn't notice the rest of their class and the tour guide leave the cave's chamber.

Craig had a feeling that they should follow the first passageway. Although it didn't have handrails like the other passageway, it was large and roomy and seemed safe enough.

Henry wanted to follow the underground stream. He had read in an encyclopedia that streams from caves often flow out of mountains or surface miles away as ponds.

Marta looked at the two passages that had handrails. She felt a slight breeze coming from one of the passages. She reminded Craig and Henry that Mr. Markum, the guide, had said that they should use only the passages that had handrails. She also pointed out that Mr. Markum had told the class that they would notice a breeze and a freshness in the air as they approached the exit. "I think we should take this passage," she announced.

Both boys agreed. In a few minutes, Henry, Craig, and Marta were outside and being greeted by their anxious classmates.

1. Why did Henry and Craig decide to follow Marta's advice?

She reminded them that the tour guide had said to stay in the marked passages and that they

would feel a breeze as they neared the exit. The passage Marta picked had these things.

_____

2. Why was Craig's suggestion rejected?

The passage Craig wanted did not have handrails. Craig's choosing the passage was based on

a feeling he had and not on sound information.

_____

3. Why was Henry's suggestion rejected?

Although Henry had read the information in a reliable source, the stream could have flowed for

miles and in places where the children could not follow.

_____

MACMILLAN PUBLISHING COMPANY

"Dangers Underground," *Landscapes* (Hardcover: pages 482-491) *Forces* (Softcover: pages 90-99)

Objective: Evaluate and make judgments *(Comprehension and Vocabulary Skills)*

Extension: Have students suggest times when the information found in an encyclopedia would be more reliable than Mr. Markum's advice.

Name   Date

A. Match each word on the left with its definition on the right. Write the letter of the definition on the line.

_b_ **1.** groping

_d_ **2.** intersection

_a_ **3.** confines

_c_ **4.** marveling

a. limits; boundaries

b. searching blindly and uncertainly

c. being or becoming filled with wonder or astonishment

d. place where things meet and cross

B. Read each sentence. Decide which word is a synonym, or has almost the same meaning, as the underlined word. Circle the letter of the word you choose.

1. At the pool's edge, Peter stood <u>gaping</u> at the white, eyeless fish that darted about.

    a. confines   **b.** groping   **c.** intersection   **(d.)** marveling

2. Ann reached out in front of her; she was <u>fumbling</u> for the flashlight she had dropped on the cave's floor.

    a. confines   **(b.)** groping   **c.** intersection   **d.** marveling

3. Jack was nervously <u>searching</u> along the cave wall for the bracket that held the torch.

    a. confines   **(b.)** groping   **c.** intersection   **d.** marveling

4. Some of the rock formations looked like waterfalls frozen within the <u>edges</u> of the cave wall.

    (a.) confines   **b.** groping   **c.** intersection   **d.** marveling

5. At the <u>crossing</u> of two passages, Nancy paused, wondering which one she should take.

    a. confines   **b.** groping   **(c.)** intersection   **d.** marveling

6. Raul was <u>gazing</u> at the enormous stalagmite and didn't notice the rest of the class leave the chamber.

    a. confines   **b.** groping   **c.** intersection   **(d.)** marveling

7. The dogs were not permitted beyond the <u>borders</u> of the yard.

    (a.) confines   **b.** groping   **c.** intersection   **d.** marveling

8. The <u>meeting</u> of the five busy streets causes much traffic controversy.

    a. confines   **b.** groping   **(c.)** intersection   **d.** marveling

"Dangers Underground," *Landscapes* (Hardcover: pages 482-491) *Forces* (Softcover: pages 90-99)

Objective: Use vocabulary words *(Comprehension and Vocabulary Skills)*

Extension: Have students write sentences for the four words listed in Part A.

137

Name _____ Date _____

A. Below are some statements about "Dangers Underground." Write **T** if the statement is true. Write **F** if the statement is false.

___T___ **1.** George Washington and his brother had found the cave.

___T___ **2.** Washington decided to explore the cave alone.

___F___ **3.** Washington told his mother where he was going.

___T___ **4.** Washington marked his route with charcoal X's.

___F___ **5.** The fish Washington found were grey with green eyes.

___T___ **6.** Washington made a wrong turn where two paths met.

___F___ **7.** Washington knew he was headed the wrong way when he saw the flock of bats.

___F___ **8.** Washington said he would never return to the cave again.

B. Below are some questions about "Dangers Underground." Write a complete sentence to answer each one. (Answers will vary.)

1. What cave animals did Washington encounter?

Washington saw white, eyeless fish; a lizard; and a flock of bats. There was also something

that slithered across his foot, perhaps a snake or another lizard.

2. What is a stalagmite?

A stalagmite is a rock formation that appears to grow from the ground up. It takes about a

hundred years for a stalagmite to grow one inch.

3. How is a stalagmite formed?

It is formed by drops of water that contain carbonic acids. The drops of water fall from the

ceiling to the cave floor, leaving tiny crystals when they dry. The crystals eventually form

the stalagmite.

4. How would you have marked your way in the cave?

_____

_____

"Dangers Underground," *Landscapes* **(Hardcover: pages 482-491)** *Forces* **(Softcover: pages 90-99)**
Objective: Demonstrate story comprehension *(Comprehension and Vocabulary Skills)*
138

Name _____ Date _____

Read each sentence. Then match the underlined word with its definition. Write the letter of the definition on the line. Note: Not every definition will be used.

___g___ **1.** It was of <u>paramount</u> importance that the spelunker mark his trail. Otherwise he would not be able to find his way out.

___c___ **2.** The spelunker used a lantern to <u>illuminate</u> the dark underground tunnel.

___i___ **3.** After carefully <u>scrutinizing</u> a map, the spelunker followed the passage to the cave's biggest room.

___k___ **4.** He found an enormous <u>chamber</u> with stalagmites climbing as high as fifty feet.

___a___ **5.** For a few moments he stood in <u>awe</u> of the spectacular sight; he had never seen anything so amazing.

___e___ **6.** Then the spelunker <u>proceeded</u> through the room to the next passageway.

___h___ **7.** He was extremely careful to avoid the shafts marked on the map; some of them <u>plummeted</u> a hundred feet or more.

___l___ **8.** The cave was a <u>labyrinth</u> of winding and connected passageways; without the map and his markings, he would be lost.

___d___ **9.** Then the spelunker came to some slabs of rock blocking the way; he could not <u>penetrate</u> them.

___j___ **10.** With some <u>reluctance</u>, the spelunker started to head back. But he would return very soon.

___n___ **11.** To him there was nothing more thrilling than the mysteries of this <u>subterranean</u> world.

a. wonder
b. little
c. light up
d. pass through
e. continued
f. eagerness
g. major
h. dropped downward
i. studying
j. unwillingness
k. room
l. maze
m. see
n. underground
o. copying

"Dangers Underground," *Landscapes* (Hardcover: pages 482-491) *Forces* (Softcover: pages 90-99)

Objective: Define words using context clues *(Comprehension and Vocabulary Skills)*

Extension: Have students write sentences for five words on this page demonstrating their understanding of the words.

139

Name _____ Date _____

A. Read the article. Use context clues to figure out the meaning of each underlined word. Write a definition for each word on the lines below.

Carlsbad Caverns National Park is a chain of subterranean caves located in southeastern New Mexico. From the moment visitors enter, there is much for them to see. At the cave's entrance, they may scrutinize the faint paintings left on the wall by Native Americans who used the cave long ago. Deep within the cavern reachable by their natural entrance or elevator, visitors can view fantastic rock formations that resemble ice castles. The stalactites and stalagmites that make up these incredible rock curtains, pillars, and icicles took thousands of years to form. No one knows of the other wonders the caverns might offer because they have not been explored in their entirety. Visitors may peer down one passage that has been explored only as far as 1,100 feet! One of the most amazing spectacle to be enjoyed is seen at dusk—hundreds of bats flying from the cave in search of insects.

1. subterranean existing below the surface of the earth

2. scrutinize to look at closely

3. incredible seemingly impossible

4. entirety state of being whole or complete

5. spectacle especially an impressive or unusual sight

B. Use the underlined words from the selection above to complete the following sentences. Write the words on the lines.

1. An _____incredible_____ underground waterfall was located deep within the cave.

2. The whole cave was too big to be seen in its _____entirety_____ in one day.

3. The scientist had to _____scrutinize_____ the rock to see the layers of mineral deposits.

4. Many caves were formed by _____subterranean_____ rivers that dissolved layers of underground rock.

5. The colored lights shining on the rocks in the cave presented an interesting _____spectacle_____.

"The Endless Cave," *Landscapes* **(Hardcover: pages 498-509)** *Forces* **(Softcover: pages 106-117)**

Objective: Define words using context clues *(Comprehension and Vocabulary Skills)*   **Extension:** Have students write sentences using the five words in Part A.

140

Name_____ Date_____

A. Read each sentence. Use the Glossary in your books to find the definition of each underlined word. Write the definition on the lines.

1. There were many rock <u>formations</u> to look at inside the cave.

   something formed or shaped
   _____

2. We dropped a penny down the <u>shaft</u> and heard it reach the bottom a long while later.

   a deep passage from ground level to an underground excavation
   _____

3. Some caves are found when miners look for a particular <u>mineral</u>.

   any natural substance that is neither animal nor vegetable and has a definite chemical

   combination
   _____

4. The six chambers are connected by a <u>system</u> of underground streams.

   a group of things or parts related or combined in such a way as to form a whole
   _____

B. Use the underlined words from the sentences above to fill in the blanks below.

   Tim and Chris Adamson peered down the old mine _____shaft_____. They nervously watched their father, who had just lowered himself into the gaping hole. Mr. Adamson worked for a mining company. He reopened

abandoned mines to try to discover new _____mineral_____ sources. While the boys waited for their father to reappear, they looked around the huge chamber that had been blasted from the rock. They inspected the small mining

trains that once traveled on a _____system_____ of tracks throughout the mine. Suddenly, Tim and Chris heard their father's voice. Boys, I found the

most incredible rock _____formations_____ in the shape of an eagle. We'll have to rename this mine *Eagle Mine.*

"The Endless Cave," *Landscapes* (Hardcover: pages 498-509) *Forces* (Softcover: pages 106-117)

Objective: Use vocabulary words *(Comprehension and Vocabulary Skills)*

Extension: Have students write a story using the following words: *shaft, mineral, formations, system.*

Name _____   Date _____

A. Below are the names of several people mentioned in "The Endless Cave." On the lines after each name, tell who the person was and how that person was important in the history of Mammoth Cave. (Answers may vary.)

1. Franklin Gorin He bought Mammoth Cave in 1838 in order to make it a tourist

attraction. He brought his sixteen-year-old slave, Steven Bishop, with him to be a guide.

_____

2. Steven Bishop He was a black slave who became a guide to Mammoth Cave.

He became famous for his explorations and discoveries in the cave. He also mapped the

known regions of the cave.

_____

3. Dr. John Croghan He bought both Mammoth Cave and Steven Bishop from Gorin.

He enlarged the hotel and got new roads built to its door. For a short time, he turned the cave

into a tuberculosis hospital.

_____

4. John Wilcox His group of explorers discovered the link between the Flint Ridge cave

system and the Mammoth Cave system to make the Mammoth-Flint Ridge cave system the

largest in the world.

_____

B. Read the following sentences. Then underline the best word in the parentheses to complete each sentence.

1. "Lost John's" body had become a mummy because of the (dry, damp), cool air in the cave.

2. The Kentucky cave wars began when George Morrison (discovered, blasted) a new entrance to Mammoth Cave.

3. On July 1, 1941, Mammoth Cave became a (state, national) park.

4. (Saltpeter, Gypsum) from Mammoth Cave was used to make gunpowder.

5. By counting the rings in one of his teeth, it was shown that Lost John was (thirty, forty-five) years old when he died.

"The Endless Cave," *Landscapes* **(Hardcover: pages 498-509)** *Forces* **(Softcover: pages 1061-117)**

Objective: Demonstrate story comprehension *(Comprehension and Vocabulary Skills)*

Name   Date

Study the prefixes and their meanings in the box below. Then fill in the circle next to the meaning of each word below.

Prefix	Meaning
un-	not
mis-	badly, incorrectly
non-	not, without
centi-	a hundred, a hundredth
deca-, deka-	ten
deci-	a tenth
kilo-	a thousand
milli-	a thousandth

1. misunderstood
- (a) not able to understand
- (c) in an understanding way
- (b) full of understanding
- (d) understand incorrectly

2. nonsense
- (a) sense badly
- (c) not sensing
- (b) without sense
- (d) full of sense

3. kilometer
- (a) one thousandth of a meter
- (c) one thousand meters
- (b) one hundred meters
- (d) one hundredth of a meter

4. decagon
- (a) having ten sides
- (c) having a hundred sides
- (b) one tenth of a side
- (d) one hundredth of a side

5. milligram
- (a) one thousand grams
- (c) one thousandth of a gram
- (b) one hundredth of a gram
- (d) one hundred grams

6. centipede
- (a) having ten legs
- (c) one tenth of a leg
- (b) having one hundred legs
- (d) one hundredth of a leg

7. decimal
- (a) a number showing tenths
- (c) a number showing hundredths
- (b) a number showing tens
- (d) a number showing thousands

"The Endless Cave," *Landscapes* (Hardcover: pages 498-509) *Forces* (Softcover: pages 106-117)

Objective: Identify prefixes: *mis-, non-, un-, centi-, deca-, deka-, deci-, kilo-, milli-* (Decoding and Phonics Skills)

Extension: Have students write the base word of each key word.

Name _____ Date _____

A. Read each definition. Then fill in the circle next to the word it defines.

1. things formed or shaped (a) myth (b) formations (c) garments
2. of poor quality (a) inferior (b) superior (c) exalted
3. higher in rank or status (a) authority (b) system (c) superior
4. melted by heat (a) molten (b) dwindled (c) inferior
5. articles of clothing (a) confines (b) garments (c) formations
6 raised in rank or position (a) superior (b) suspended (c) exalted
7. became gradually smaller (a) exalted (b) dwindled (c) suspended
8. limits; boundaries (a) confines (b) garments (c) intersection
9. a deep passage (a) defy (b) procession (c) shaft
10. place where things meet and cross (a) system (b) intersection (c) shaft

B. Read the sentences. Then fill in the circle next to the word that best completes each sentence.

1. The beliefs of the ancient Greeks have been told in many a/an _____.
   (a) procession (b) authority (c) myth

2. To them, the great forces of nature were gods who had complete _____.
   (a) superior (b) authority (c) system

3. Anyone who dared to _____ the gods would be punished severely.
   (a) defy (b) exalted (c) shaft

4. Each year the Greeks held a/an _____ through the streets of the city in honor of the gods.
   (a) intersection (b) garments (c) procession

5. Although we no longer believe in nature gods, we are constantly _____ at the forces of nature at work.
   (a) suspended (b) marveling (c) groping

6. We spent years _____ for answers to the mysteries of nature's forces.
   (a) groping (b) marveling (c) dwindling

7. Some questions about the earth's complex _____ of natural forces remain unanswered.
   (a) intersection (b) mineral (c) system

Cumulative Vocabulary Review

Objective: Use vocabulary words *(Comprehension and Vocabulary Skills)*

Extension: Have students choose three pairs of words and write a sentence using each pair.

Level 11, Unit 1   ENTERPRISES

Kid Power

1	2	3	4	5

You Can Get A Job!

6	7	8	9

The Doughnut Machine

10	11	12	13

Skills Activity

14

The Toothpaste Millionaire

15	16	17	18

Cumulative Vocabulary Review

19

Skills Activity

20

Henry Reed's Journal

21	22	23	24

Skills Activity

25

Children's Express

26	27	28	29

Mysteriously Yours, Maggie Marmelstein

30	31	32	33

Cumulative Vocabulary Review

34

Level 11, Unit 2   FRONTIERS

Diablo Blanco

35	36	37	38

Going West

39	40	41	42

Skills Activity

43

By the Shores of Silver Lake

44	45	46	47	48

The Art of the Old West

49	50	51	52

Cumulative Vocabulary Review

53

Caddie Woodlawn

54	55	56	57

Frontier Schools

58	59	60	61

Skills Activity

62

Women of the West

63	64	65	66	67

Saved by a Whisker

68	69	70	71

Cumulative Vocabulary Review

72

Level 11, Unit 3

The Night of the Leonids

| 73 | 74 | 75 | 76 |

The House of Dies Drear

| 77 | 78 | 79 | 80 |

Skills Activity

| 81 |

A Game of Catch

| 82 | 83 | 84 | 85 |

Canyon Winter

| 86 | 87 | 88 | 89 |

Cumulative Vocabulary Review

| 90 |

Skills Activity

| 91 |

C.L.U.T.Z.

| 92 | 93 | 94 | 95 |

The Flight of Icarus

| 96 | 97 | 98 | 99 |

Skills Activity

| 100 |

East of the Sun and West of the Moon

| 101 | 102 | 103 | 104 | 105 |

Cumulative Vocabulary Review

| 106 |

Level 11, Unit 4

Float Down the Tamarack

| 107 | 108 | 109 | 110 |

The Changing River

| 111 | 112 | 113 | 114 | 115 |

Skills Activity

| 116 |

The Big Wave

| 117 | 118 | 119 | 120 |

Skills Activity

| 121 |

Mount St. Helens

| 122 | 123 | 124 | 125 |

Cumulative Vocabulary Review

| 126 |

Skills Activity

| 127 |

A Strange Sled Race

| 128 | 129 | 130 | 131 |

Dorothy's Journey to the Center of the Earth

| 132 | 133 | 134 | 135 |

Dangers Underground

| 136 | 137 | 138 | 139 |

The Endless Cave

| 140 | 141 | 142 | 143 |

Cumulative Vocabulary Review

| 144 |